MEMORY LANE
a Second Look

A collection of pictorial memories
of Leeds from the archives of the

YORKSHIRE Evening Post

The Breedon Books
Publishing Company
Derby

First published in Great Britain by
The Breedon Books Publishing Company Limited
Breedon House, 44 Friar Gate, Derby, DE1 1DA.
1999

ISBN 1 85983 150 8

Printed and bound by Butler & Tanner Ltd., Selwood Printing Works,
Caxton Road, Frome, Somerset.

Colour separations and jacket printing by GreenShires Ltd, Leicester.

Contents

Acknowledgements

The compiler/author of this book received considerable assistance from people in all walks of life in preparing the material it contains, and wishes to express his grateful thanks. If any are missed from the following list, he hopes they will allow him to blame his 'failing shorthand' and the usual 'advancing years' for their absence.

The staff of the Yorkshire Post Newspapers Library and the YPN Photographic Department, Peter Stainthorpe, Ewart W. Clay, Malcolm G. Barker, Don Cole, the noted North Leeds historian; and Ron Hartley, Manager of the Horsforth Village Museum.

He also records his particular thanks to his wife, Joyce, for her help with research; and for her patience when, for a period, our home was turned into a cross between a reference library and a photographic studio.

The majority of pictures in this book are from the Library or Photographic Department of Yorkshire Post Newspapers and the publishers are grateful for permission to use them. Sources of other pictures are acknowledged in the captions.

Photographic Purchases

Anyone interested in purchasing copies of photographs belonging to Yorkshire Post Newspapers, please contact the Yorkshire Post Photo Sales Department. Telephone: 0113-243-2701. Ext. 1360. Please quote this publication and state on which page the photograph appears.

Foreword

THE GENTLEMAN who wrote the Foreword to the original *Memory Lane, Leeds 1*, published just three years ago recorded that as a young journalist, Allen Rowley had a reputation among his colleagues for finding a different angle in a story. Well, I have to say he has done it again, for few books written about Leeds have uncovered so many little-known facts about the city; brought out the warmth of the true 'Loiners' or been able to establish some sort of balance between those who vote for change and those who make valiant efforts to retain various structures and features.

An ever-ready touch of humour helps to keep this new volume close to the lives and interests of the ordinary people; something which is often lost in more staid accounts. His different, but highly-perceptive approach to various aspects of city life and development over the years also makes a refreshing change from some more academic accounts.

The introduction, and a detailed explanation of what they reveal, of aerial pictures of the city taken at different periods of time, not only underline the author's long-time aviation experience but, to the reader unaccustomed to seeing his or her city from above, these provide a fascinating new look at Leeds and clearly illustrate many of the changes which have taken place.

Mr Rowley is not, of course, merely stirring the memories of his own generation. The able and willing assistance of those he likes to call his 'elders', including his 99-year-old mother-in-law, has helped to unearth facts and figures regarding long-vanished points of interest; or of re-sited items which members of the younger generation might well pass every day without having the slightest idea of their once important standing in the community.

He himself admits to having been carried away by 'period atmosphere' after lengthy efforts to discover how sections of the older, near-400 pictures in the book could be identified. In one case, it was a gatepost on a 130-year-old photograph of a rural scene which he was finally able to track down – still standing amidst the hurly-burly of what is now one of the city's busiest arterial roads.

Many 'Leeds Loiners' will be surprised at what scores of these pictures reveal, and they will bring many memories; some a little sad, others absolutely happy, and many of the stuff of which they can be made proud.

Councillor Brian Walker
Leader of the Council

Leeds – a reintroduction

MEMORY, impressions, change, education: in selecting some 400 photographs for use in this publication, then carrying-out the research required to write some 400 captions, plus extended explanations to put the reader 'in the picture' (no pun intended), those four words at the start of this reintroduction have never been far from my mind. One of the descriptions of 'memory' in *The New Imperial Reference Dictionary* reads: '…time within which past things can be remembered.' If 'time' in this sense means the opportunity to sit back in one's retirement and think of events/places/people encountered in one's past; then I have to confess to sometimes uttering the oft-heard cry of many 'retired' people: "There's so much to do, I don't know how I found time to go out to work."

But then, I am fortunate in that much of the work I do in my 'retirement' differs but little from what I did in full-time employment. So the dictionary explanation covers two situations, for memories were certainly stirred by the research involved in producing these captions.

As for 'impressions' – perhaps the biggest one is just how far we have come in my own 72 years. The Leeds I knew as a teenager, on fairly regular visits, has not changed out of all recognition, as some are wont to claim. But parts of it have got pretty near the point where it is possible, as I have tried to show in sections of this volume, that they have changed not once but several times, so that traces of the original site/scene/structure have been wiped-out for ever.

Which brings us to the word 'change' and much of that is self-evident in many of these pictures; and as per the examples of grandparents and parents who have taken grandchildren and children to see parts of the city where they themselves were born and grew up, only to find that the entire landscape has felt the weight of successive teams of demolition and reconstruction workers to the point where it is now impossible to establish where their homes/factories/local pub or what-have-you used to stand.

So I hope this second volume of *Memory Lane* will also be of some 'educational' value – to quote the last of the four introductory words – for old and young alike. I can take them pretty near to their roots through these pictures, but cannot resurrect what the bulldozers have ground into the earth and the steel erectors and masons built upon; sometimes several times.

When I wrote the previous edition, I was determined to give the reader a much better insight into the many photographs than the all-too-easy throw-away one, or two-liners used by all too many compilers of such publications e.g. "A 1920s view of the High Street looking east", followed by a 'different' picture with a 'different' caption: "A 1920s view of the High Street looking west." I think the reader deserves much more, and any compiler worth his or her salt should be determined to give more.

Toward that end, and somewhat remarkably in this high-tech age, the squeezing of much valuable information out of many pictures used here was achieved by the use of a simple large magnifying glass. This magnification often made all the difference between a short caption regarding (say) "Harry Bloggins' shop at the corner of High Street and Gasworks Terrace" and the intriguing revelation of what was in the shop window – style, selection, cost, period etc. And after all, isn't that what the ladies, bless 'em, go to look at …not the shop front?

So I hope there is an informative education factor here too; and an all-round impression of what things were really like; and in the alleys alongside the shops as well as in their windows!

In producing a book about a city, it is a comparatively easy task to concentrate on the 'Up Front' image: main buildings, streets and infrastructure. True, something of that nature is required, but in this second volume I have moved the focus somewhat, especially on to the people who really make the city tick; and not least the suburbs, so often much-maligned by the alleged intelligentsia and chattering classes.

We can see city folk here in all their moods and situations: in the hovels that made-up the slums, in conditions which made life miserable for countless housewives. Nevertheless, most braved the conditions and did their best, and oft-produced families that were a credit to them. We can see here what they did in the all-too-brief periods that went for leisure time: street parties and games, charabanc trips, the magic of the 'twopenny rush' at the 'pictures' and nights out at theatres which were second-to-none outside of London. There are tales of tragedy at school and the joy of the Roundhay Park 'Children's Days' of blessed memory. If you are a true 'Loiner' then you, or certainly your older relatives and friends, have experienced the 'goings on' caught by photographers who, themselves, did not know then that they were making an important contribution to the city's history.

And we can see the better-off, a goodly number of

which "came up from nowt," as the old Yorkshire saying went: and there are well-known names here whose endeavours made them, and Leeds, famous the world over.

Even so, there is still time and the opportunity, for the city and its people to go further – and on the day I write this the *Yorkshire Post* has published a special section on Regional Development in which a leading merchant banker says Leeds has eclipsed Manchester and is now the most significant financial player in the UK apart from London.

Perhaps my most enduring memory of researching and writing these two volumes is of how, in dealing with 'the past' for day after day, week-after-week, one can almost be transported back in time …almost seeing and hearing ancient sights and sounds; until the introductory music of the late night television news brings one crashing, not entirely happily, back to the present.

In particular, I recall spending a whole week delving into photographs, newspaper cuttings, books, facts and figures relating to an area bounded by Eastgate, Marsh Lane, Leeds Parish Church and the Markets area. The following Sunday morning I rose earlier than usual and walked through that area, feeling almost as if I was in some kind of twisted time warp …yes, Appleyard's unique filling station building was still there; so was the fortress-like Millgarth police station, a picture of whose predecessor had taken weeks to unearth. Across the road was the area where Quarry Hill Flats once dominated the landscape – but only for around a quarter of a century – and now there are state of the art redevelopments.

Yet someone has seen fit to leave an open area where grass, trees, bushes and flowers, actually grow in the general area where, back in 1745, S. & N. Buck sat on a grassy bank and made that drawing of the city which forms the first illustration in this new volume; thus taking us back if not to the roots, then to the early development of parts of Leeds which still stand.

A timely consideration, I think, as we go through the last year of a century, of which much is mirrored within these covers. I wonder how many times it will change again before 2099?

Allen Rowley,
Leeds
May 1999

This large, rich and populous town…

This delightful view of Leeds in 1745 was one of a famous series of drawings made of castles and towns throughout the land by S. and N. Buck in the early 18th century. Their standpoint is believed to have been on the rising ground east of the city centre in the area of Richmond Hill.

Looking upstream, the River Aire runs from the bottom left-hand corner up to Leeds Bridge – then the only crossing in this area. The Parish Church is to the right of the bridge, with the spire of Trinity Church (rarely missing from any central Leeds view), to its right.

There is meadow land and a large market garden over to the right, towards Vicar Lane and today's Eastgate. The open fields on the rolling hills in the distance run from Armley on the left across Woodhouse, Headingley, Beckett Park, West Park, to the distant Tinshill.

Although parts of the description of Leeds printed below the view are faded in parts, magnification has allowed most of it to be reproduced here.

This picture was, incidentally, taken by Planet News Ltd, on 3 April 1962, especially for the *Yorkshire Post*. At that time the drawing was at the Parker Gallery in London's Albemarle Street and was due to be exhibited at a forthcoming Antique Dealers Fair.

Here's what the description says (and is reproduced exactly):

This large, rich and populous town is situate almost in the West Riding of Yorkshire, the navigable River Aire divides the Town into two parts which are rejoined by a spacious Stone Bridge, formerly remarkable for the Mixt Cloth Markets being held upon it but the Increase of Trade rendering it incommodious for passengers, the Market was removed by Act of Parliament in 1684 to the East side of the Bridge gate (or in the Dialect of the Country Brig-gate) where it is yet held in so much increas'd that on a moderate Computation upwards of 3000 Clothiers expose their manufactures to sale there every Thursday and Saturday in the open air, the Clothes being laid on trestles neatly ranged for the purpose, the time for the market is limited for one hour and begins in summer time at 6 o'Clock in the morning and in the winter as soon as the Merchants can see to distinguish the Colours, the Signal being given by the Ringing of a Bell at an Old Chappel at the Bridge feet, which rings again at the expiration of the hour. It is almost incredible to tell what large sums of money are laid out every Market Day in so short a space of time and that with so profound audience as surprises all Strangers. The Market is allowed to be the largest in England for Bread and Cloths, which are exported from hence to Germany, Italy, Spain, Portugal and even to the most remote places of the known world. There is besides the Market for mixt Cloth already mentioned a hand some well built hall for the White Cloth under which are very Convenient Cells where the Clothiers may deposit the Cloth remaining unsold from one market day to another. This market is kept only on Tuesdays in the afternoon and continues likewise the space of one hour. This Town was very populous even in the time of the Saxons and the Residence of one of The Kings of Northumberland. West from the Bridge upon an easy Ascent stood a famous castle with a park adjoining which contains the name of the Park to this day. This castle was besieged by Stephen in long march toward Scotland Anno 1139. Richard II lodged here some time. Here are three stately churches viz. St Peter's commonly called the old church, a plain and very spacious building. St John's founded, finished and liberally endowed by Harrison Esq., a native who provided a house for the Minister and built a Chappel, Alms Houses, Free School and Market Cross at his own expense.

The New Church, or Trinity was built by subscription and endowed with lands to the value of … (at this point a different set of handwriting appears to take over the script and even with magnification has proved indecipherable.

Civic Pride

In this day and age where a veritable deluge of political news is poured into the ears; and before the eyes of radio and television listeners and viewers, it will come as no surprise to learn that a century ago the equivalent of today's spin doctors were constantly seeking ways and means of 'putting one across' rival parties. Pictured here is the face of a medal struck by the Leeds Tories in 1896 to mark the election of the first Tory Lord Mayor of the city for 60 years. The difference between the two heads does not indicate how that individual had aged in the intervening period: the mayor is on the left, his deputy on the right. One might be forgiven for feeling that this piece would not win first prize in the Civic Hall's magnificent collection of official gifts and civic regalia.

From the outset the Leeds city fathers (does one have to add 'mothers,' too, in this PC-age?) set out to impress visitors – especially those from the south – that theirs was no hick town out on the tundra and it had the history, will, spirit and know-how to allow it to compete for fame, and results, with any place its size south of a line from Bristol to the Wash, and more particularly west of the Pennines.

Over the past three centuries it has produced some striking and much-admired architecture, both civic and privately-developed, which has attracted much praise and certainly proved that the brass earned amidst the muck of mills and mines to the west, south and east of the rapidly-growing town could be well-spent on things that would add to civic pride.

Not least among them is the Civic Mace, pictured here, which dates back to the 17th century.

Years ago, Leeds had three large tricorne ostrich feather hats from which a Lord Mayor could choose when it was necessary to wear a head covering on a ceremonial occasion. Miss J. B. Kitson, the first woman Lord Mayor of Leeds, was unabashed at wearing such headgear when she took office, but did exercise some female feelings by having the feathers removed.

In 1958, when Alderman Mrs Mary Pearce became the city's second woman Lord Mayor, she took things a stage further and decided on 'something more suitable for a Lady Lord Mayor'.

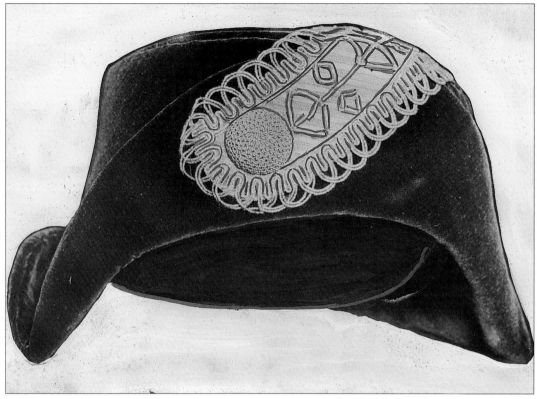

Made by a Leeds milliner her hat, pictured here, was in effect almost a tricorne in reverse. The ceremonial near-chapeau was in black velvet with the straight part to the front instead of at the back. The gold cockade was across the front instead of at the side.

Some of the lads on the council are reported to have been told to desist from making cracks about 'Madame Bonaparte' though Mrs Pearce would, no doubt, have taken it in good part…

During the height of the Cold War, the balloon almost went up over the shooting down of an American U2 spy plane flown by one Gary Powers.

Leeds was one up on the Americans because it owned U1 although, as you can see from this picture, it was hardly likely to go near-supersonic over Russia.

U1 has been the registration number carried by the official cars of a string of Leeds Lord Mayors and this one was the very first. Then a private car, one of a comparative few in the city, it was owned by the late Mr Currer Briggs, the city's Lord Mayor at the turn of the century.

This picture does not make it clear whether Mr Briggs had lost his way in Adel Woods or was presenting long service medals to gardeners at Temple Newsam.

What is clear is that he had come prepared for all eventualities: with a spare tyre and petrol can strapped on the roof.

Proof of the handing-down of the U1 registration lies in this picture, taken 73 years after the previous one, with the Lord Mayor's civic Daimler leaving London's Royal Garden Hotel.

But what was the vehicle doing nearly 200 miles away from home? Perhaps the Lord Mayor had been to see off a Mr Frank Lush, from Kent, who had written offering to sell his Rolls-Royce, bearing the number plate U2, to Leeds. He said it was valued at £12,500 but would be willing to accept £10,000. His offer was turned down.

Talk about after the Lord Mayor's Show ...the paragraph containing the above tit-bit in the Council Report in the *Yorkshire Evening Post* of 7 July 1973, is followed by another reading: 'Wetherby's modernised public lavatories in The Shambles have been described as the best in the county. Councillor Harold Oates told Wetherby Rural Council: "I have been stopped by several ladies and they tell me they are the best loos in Yorkshire".'

Yes, the civic heads and citizens of Leeds have their pride, but it seems someone was carrying it a bit far when they approved the placing of this stylised version of the city's coat-of-arms on one of the metal spans under the Whitehall Road Bridge. After all, this isn't Venice y'know, although an old *YEP* sub-editor who was a constant critic of the airport did once say that more tourists arrived in Leeds by canal barge than ever landed at the then Leeds-Bradford Airport. Arty Venetians would, no doubt, have considered this design to be a wolf in sheep's clothing...

The collection of Leeds civic silver, referred to above, was enhanced in May 1968, by the presentation of this striking figure of Mercury, emblem of the Royal Signals, by the 49th (Yorkshire) Signal Regiment (TA) to mark the conferment of the freedom of the city on the regiment.

In 1979, the well-known Leeds china shop – Doyle Ltd – of Albion Street, and the Leeds Junior Chamber of Commerce got together to commission a limited edition (200) of The Leeds Plate (pictured). Produced by Caverswall, of Stoke on Trent, it was designed by artist John Ball.

It centred on the Leeds coat-of-arms with five cameos around the border featuring the Town Hall, Civic Hall, Parish Church, Kirkstall Abbey and Templenewsam House, with the white rose of Yorkshire standing proud from the intricate border tapestry. They sold then for £50 apiece.

Needless to say, the commissioning body would not have dared perpetrate the boob committed by a famous international mail order house which, in 1998, managed to include a cameo of Leeds Castle, Kent, on a plate intended for sale in Yorkshire.

People who have pondered just what floor covering should grace the hallways of their homes, having over the years considered lino, lino tiles, wood blocks, plain carpet, patterned carpet, carpet tiles or what have you, might well have blanched at the thought of meeting the requirements of the vast space in the entrance of Leeds Civic Hall.

And as if the space problems were not enough, there were the political aspects to consider: too much red would raise the ire of the blues and vice versa.

But it seems that whoever stuck his, or her, neck out in choosing the new carpet in 1973 hit on the one theme that seems to suit all sides – nothing less than the city's coat-of-arms.

Guests at a 'At Home' held by the then Lady Mayoress (Mrs Kenneth Travis Davison) in July that year, were among the early ratepayers who had the chance to examine what their money had purchased and it seems most of them proclaimed they were delighted; but then, it was a free tea.

Here the Lady Mayoress (centre), her daughter, Caroline (kneeling) and the Deputy Lady Mayoress, Mrs George Somers, wait for the guests to move forward and make their marks upon this noble pattern.

Around the City Centre

Albion Street

Because it was located near the centre of what some referred to as the 'square mile' of the city centre's shopping district, the front office of the *Yorkshire Post* and *Yorkshire Evening Post*, at the corner of Bond Street and Albion Street (opposite what is now Boots), was a popular meeting place and affectionately known to the staff as 'The old lady of Albion Street'. It fronted about a dozen buildings behind those to the right and left of this photograph including the house of the company's first vice-chairman.

But in the early 1960s, expansion of business and ever-increasing traffic, impeding delivery vans, led to a search for new premises with the present Wellington Street site being acquired in October 1967. The topping-out ceremony on the new building was performed by the then chairman, the late Sir Kenneth Parkinson, on 30 October 1969.

That incredible weekend move from Albion Street to Wellington Street was begun as the *Evening Post* finished its last press run at the former site at about 6 pm on Saturday, 26 September, and the transfer of staff and equipment was achieved in time for the *Yorkshire Post* to be printed at the latter site for Monday morning readers. It was an achievement which still brings "how did we ever do it?" questions to the minds of the steadily-decreasing number of those of us who took part. But did it we did: and within half a day we had also established which West End pubs would be our new 'locals'…

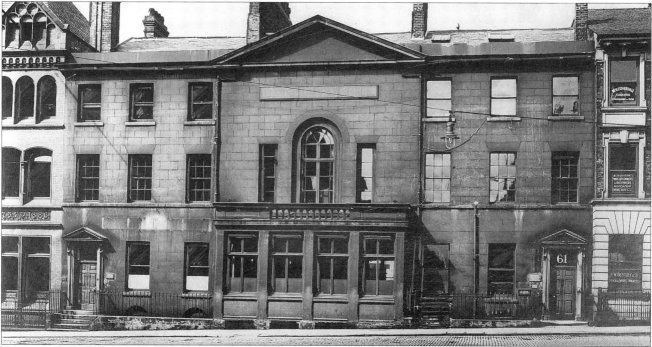

Pictured back in 1927, the Leeds Stock Exchange was just up the street and next door to the *Yorkshire Post* buildings, the edge of which can be seen below the gable on the left. A stone relief above the two lower windows of the *YP* building reads 1754-1886 which, as every reader knows (because it is imprinted on the Leader page on every publication day), are the dates when the *Yorkshire Post* was founded – as the *Leeds Intelligencer* on 2 July 1754 and became a daily – the *Yorkshire Post* – on 2 July 1866. The stone relief does not, however, record the date when the *YP* absorbed the *Leeds Mercury* (founded 1718) in November 1939.

The old Stock Exchange had seen its share of successes and failures; although the balcony probably wasn't high enough to make for a successful suicide in the case of the latter. But a bank did once go bust there. And a famous Leeds firm of solicitors, which later owned the building, founded its fortunes there. A court couturier, Madame Pierce, once sold sumptuous apparel to the toffs on the first floor.

By the 1960s, the building had lost its balcony, but anyone wanting to play the markets could find it more easily, thanks to a bold sign which, some sniffed, spoiled the Georgian frontage. The alterations which brought the shops had come about in 1928 and in the closing years of this block, the well-known names (from left to right) of Martins the Cleaners, Waldens the Bedding Specialists and L. Pobjee, Florist and Fruiterer, did good business there – not least thanks to the staffs of the *Yorkshire Post* and *Yorkshire Evening Post* who were scattered through the dozen or so buildings between the Albion Street frontage and the distant Upper Basinghall Street. Take a picture from this same spot today and the sky would be blocked out by the multi-storeys of West Riding House.

It is hard to imagine that this corner shop – bearing enough signs for pipes, Henry Irving cigars, cigarettes, tobacco pouches and pipe repairs – to give today's average doctor heart failure, stood on the corner where Albion Street – running off to the left; met Guildford Street (running off to the right), which is now part of The Headrow. It's a lovely bright morning in 1906 and the postman is on his rounds. A well-known local name – Taylors' Drug Company, was advertising its Photographic Showroom on the extreme right; above the shop of J. Easby, British and Foreign Fruiterer. Incidentally, the tobacconist also repaired sticks: they really set out to serve in those days…

His shop occupied a historic site, for at one time the Burley Bar Stone, marking the edge of the town stood here. On The Headrow wall of the Leeds and Holbeck Building Society block which now stands here (just to the right of the corner door of the former tobacco shop), there is a Leeds Civic Trust plaque reading: 'Burley Bar Stone (now inside the main Leeds and Holbeck Society), marked the medieval boundary between the manoral borough, or town of Leeds, and Leeds Main Riding, the surround agricultural land. First Recorded 1725.'

There was just a touch of continental atmosphere about the old Leeds Co-operative Society building, on the east side of Albion Street, near the bottom. Cobbles, a bassinet, full skirts, neat and tidy pavement; it was a tower of respectability; all this and 'divi' too! Can you remember your check number…? But this is all gone: "It's summat called a precinct now Priscilla, no traffic and all that …mind that van doesn't knock you down…"

Briggate

Not the busiest of days in Briggate in this turn-of-the-century view. Probably still the city's most popular street in shopping terms, it never had quite the architectural style of The Headrow, once the latter had been opened-up from what had been little more than a lane. But the mix of Briggate's buildings has been of little concern to shoppers who, for well over a century, have come from far and wide to find bargains in fashions, shoes, food shops, and general emporiums. The street's outsize gas lamps are worthy of note; transport fans will note that the electric trams had still to arrive (the one in the centre was steam-hauled). Males who went for a pint whilst their ladies did the shopping knew exactly where the railing-protected steps led to beneath the road and, as in most pictures of the period, 95% of the males wore a cap or hat. Note the watch chain across the waistcoat of the chap crossing on the left: it was big enough to tie-up a moderately-sized boat on Roundhay's Waterloo Lake.

An artist's impression of this section of Briggate appeared in the first volume of *Memory Lane* and included the Albion Hotel, built in 1824. It was rebuilt 50 years later in the rather striking style shown here. Its total life spanned just over 100 years for, as the posters on its windows and on the property on the left reveal in this 1927 photo, the premises had been acquired by no less than F. W. Woolworth & Co Ltd, as one of its 'Threepenny and Sixpenny Stores'. Their new building went up on the site in 1928 and they remained there until they moved to the Merrion Centre in the 1980s. The sale of the Albion site also involved the LNER premises on the left, where a large cup displayed in the window indicated they were doing something right. Today's train operating companies please note…

Across the road from the Albion stood the rather splendid Imperial Hotel, which an architectural correspondent once described as 'chateau-like'. Certainly, it would not have looked out of place in the area around New York's Times Square of that period, nor in one of the gracious streets of Paris. However, its death knell was sounded in 1957 when Montague Burton Ltd, the multiple tailors who had a large shop at ground floor level on the site, put forward a plan for redevelopment. Following a fully-expected tussle with Leeds Corporation, the Minister of Housing and Local Government allowed Burton's appeal and by the 1960s the Imperial was no more.

City Square

As described earlier, the cloth markets originally held on Leeds Bridge overflowed to the point where extra space had to be found. One answer was the Coloured Cloth Hall erected in 1756-58 on the site where the Post Office now stands on the West side of City Square. The Rotunda was added about 1780, making the complex one of the largest of its type in Europe.

The task of keeping the Coloured Cloth Hall in good order fell to caretakers whose family portrait this is. They were the last people to undertake that job, for Leeds Corporation purchased the premises in 1889 at a sum in excess of £60,000 with a view to carrying-out improvements in the area. They were the first of a series, which have seen the face of City Square change several times over the years. Sites for advertisements were keenly sought-after in the Square (see Volume One) and, as ever in the old days, health cures were often predominant. Among the bills plastered on the Cloth Hall wall were these, printed exactly as displayed: 'A cup of pure & healthy cocoa for a farthing.' 'When your honour's at STEAK, try the YORKSHIRE RELISH, it is unimpeachable.' 'Toulson's Precious Tig Drops Cures Neuralgia.'

Time marches on and City Square is taking on that sense of importance which has developed over the years. In this post-World War One view, electric trams have arrived; although hand-barrows, and horses and carts still hold their share of the transport business. Ice cream wars show signs of breaking out as the carts of rival vendors are parked beside the central island on the left. There isn't a single motor vehicle in sight, but the alarm bells should be ringing in the clock tower where, above the second floor windows of the building it dominates, the badge and initials of the AA have appeared to usher in the age of breakdown assistance (with a salute thrown-in by the patrolman in those dutiful days). In the background on the right is the old Queens Hotel; in the foreground is the war memorial with 'Winged Victory' peacefully poised before being despatched on her sad and sorry wanderings around the city. What a shame that she and the memorial could not have been assured of a permanent home in this place where more people would have got her message. Perhaps even the vandals who, instead, chose to desecrate this memorial to the fallen when it was moved to the Garden of Rest in The Headrow. It is sad to think that some members of the bomber crews the memorial honours were no older than the skate-boarding morons who have chosen to damage it in recent years.

Commercial Street

Countless Yorkshire ladies and just as many lady visitors from elsewhere, long regarded tea at Betty's Café on the corner of Land's Lane and Commercial Street, as a sophisticated break amidst the hurly-burly of a day's shopping in the city. Its well-proportioned frontage and bay windows affording a superior view of the goings-on down below, and made it a haven of rest that was a cut above the rest. But what was there before the café? Well, here it is – and just try to imagine the shock/horror of all those ladies had they known. At least, that is what the faded caption suggests. It is hard to imagine just what 'Fine Art' was for sale through that doorway indicated by the sign. "And as for those dreadful advertisements, my dear Penelope, why – just look at them: Zebra grate polish; Goodall's Custard Powder; Kompo for colds and, my goodness – I nearly had a touch of the vapours when I perceived it …a girl in a bathing dress with one leg (ahem!) bare to just above the knee. What is the world coming to, my dear?" What indeed – and Channel Four hadn't even been thought of in those days…

Almost as surprising as the revelation in the previous picture of what part of Commercial Street used to be like, is this structure also in that street, which cost the compiler almost as much time and effort in trying to discover just why it was erected, as he experienced in trying to identify the location of Charley Cake Park (see the 'Parks-a-Plenty' section of this volume). Perhaps the worthy constable beneath the arch was there for a purpose: to prevent people turning it into an early version of a take-away; or eating it on the spot? Enough of the teasing: it was erected by Hy.Child, proprietor of the Mitre Hotel, to mark the visit to Leeds of the Duke and Duchess of York on 5 October 1894, and given the grand title: Triumphal Arch of Bread. Hundreds of loaves, of various shapes and sizes, went into its construction and it was topped and trimmed with sheaves of wheat. Anyone fancy a sandwich…?

If only because he and his fellow young journalists were apt to use the men only Mitre Hotel and restaurant for its reasonably-priced meals and well-kept ale back in the 1950s, the compiler found himself at home with this – and the previous photograph of the hotel. In the picture with the 'Bread Arch', the Mitre (built in 1907 on the site of the old Horse and Jockey, which had a tradition dating back to 1774), has a front wall extending each side of the arch and the advert painted on the chimney stack on the left indicates the hotel went back some distance from Commercial Street. By the 1950s, however, the only evidence of the Mitre was this doorway, leading to a marble-walled staircase which descended to the basement bar and restaurant with its splendid woodwork, partitioned cubicles and Victorian-type stove. A well-known personality for more than 40 years was the Italian head waiter, Ettore Martelli, who retired in 1950. On the closing night, in March 1961, his successor, 67-year-old Harold Blackburn, commented: "We seem to be losing touch with the English way of life as we used to know it – you cannot recapture atmosphere and tradition." "We'll drink to that," said what remains of that crowd of once young journos, when they were shown a picture of that farewell night.

Cookridge Street

Had he been around to take a stroll up Cookridge Street in 1985, Cuthbert Brodrick, the young architect from Hull who designed Leeds Town Hall (built in the 1850s) might have wept, or become apoplectic when he saw this somewhat distressed set of buildings opposite the Civic Theatre. They did nothing to enhance the Civic Hall in the background. It is hard to believe that they were ever allowed to get into this state, and a sigh of relief must have gone up from the various bodies keen on the preservation of Leeds buildings when they were advertised as a 'refurbishment opportunity' toward the end of 1985. For these were no less than 'Brodrick's Shops', designed by the chap who had planned that internationally-famous town hall less than a few hundred yards away.

Happily for all concerned, the refurbishment challenge was taken-up and the buildings were restored to a condition that Cuthbert would have found satisfactory. Pity about the position of the street lamp, however. On the extreme left, the back wall of Cuthbert's masterpiece can be seen in the distance; on the extreme right, round the corner, a plaque (what a shame it was not positioned on the front wall) from Leeds Civic Trust records: 'These fine shops and offices were designed by Cuthbert Brodrick (1822-1905), the architect of Leeds Town Hall, the Corn Exchange and the Mechanics Institute. They were renovated by Trinity Services in 1988. Erected 1864.'

Dark Arches

The increase in pleasure craft coming into the Leeds area and the consequent development of the Canal Basin, along with the shopping area and craft markets at Granary Wharf, have tended to disperse the air of mystery which, for years, surrounded the area which, had Leeds been in the USA, would almost certainly have been referred to as 'south of the railroad tracks'. For although those now familiar with the district tend to believe it was a channelled watercourse which brought it all about; in fact it was the railway.

The years of 'Railway Mania', saw various companies striving to become the first to establish a major terminal in the centre of the city. One station, if built, would have stretched some 900ft from Monk Bridge, south of the city centre, to where Infirmary Street is today. Another would have required a viaduct to have been built across the busy city centre, roughly in line with where Boar Lane runs. In fact the honour went to the Wellington Station of the Leeds and Bradford Railway (incorporated 4 July 1844) which was tucked away at the east end of Wellington Street, near the site of the original Queen's Hotel (pictured in the earlier view of City Square).

All the station builders' plans had to contend with the River Aire which split the city north and south. A complex set of underground channels and spillways finally allowed Leeds City Station, as it eventually became known, to be constructed over some ten acres on a massive set of viaducts beneath which were …The Dark Arches.

Looking like some film set where Harrison Ford would have been well and truly at home, the tunnels and spillways which carry the river are below the level of the large arches which support the railway viaduct; the station platforms and various other structures. Pictured on a quiet day with a gentle flow through which the tunnel floor can be seen, one of the tunnels also reveals amidst its stone and brick facing plenty of patching where the water and assorted debris has thundered through when in full spate. All this whilst the piano and tea cups tinkled in the Queens Hotel Lounge not too far overhead!

Duncan Street

Although the building straight ahead is well-known to most Leeds citizens, most readers might well be baffled by the building graced by large columns on the left. It was the Central Market, built at the junction of Duncan Street and New Market Street in 1824-27. It was the first large 'covered' market in the city centre, with over 50 stalls for fruit and vegetables, and dairy produce. Around the first floor a bazaar was arranged, dealing in fancy goods. At street level on the outside there were over 60 shops, many occupied by butchers and fishmongers.

The market's striking appearance alone was a cause of much pride for the citizenry and its covered facilities were a big attraction for people travelling from surrounding areas. Sadly, it was gutted by fire on 21 June 1895. Note the single tram track running through the sea of cobbles and the single-deck horse-drawn tram. In the background, for someone obviously better off, is a hansom cab.

By 1901 high-tech tramway equipment was being enjoyed by the residents of thoroughly modern Leeds. In this busy transport scene, looking along Duncan Street from the corner of Boar Lane, with Lower Briggate in the right foreground, a steam-powered tram was about to start its dash for Wortley. Pedestrians were being encouraged to try Andrews Liver Salts by the poster on its double-deck passenger trailer. Close behind is another of the formidable steam cars with a single-decker in tow. But the real high-tech stuff is on the left where an electric tram is affording passengers a crisp, snowy morning view from its open top deck. As in any other pictures of this crossing in those years, jay walkers are ploughing their courses to every point of the compass. And a poor soul well-known to passers-by, is on his knees begging on the pavement edge of Lower Briggate.

Things had brightened-up considerably in Duncan Street by 1937. There is a definite big city air about this photo, looking toward Boar Lane, and had John Prescott been around, he would have been delighted to note that public transport vehicles just about out-numbered private cars. Names fixed in the memories of Leeds folk now aged 60 to 100 adorn trams and buildings: Burton, Saxone, Melbourne Ales, the *Leeds Mercury* and, not to be left out, the *Yorkshire Evening Post* on the half a tram seen on the extreme left. As ever, Trinity Church spire tops it all yet again.

That spire is back again in this picture of 16 June 1944, the day before the author's birthday, shortly before he prepared to leave his Army Cadet Force uniform behind and don full-blown real army khaki and go off to help finish-off Hitler. All the ladies in view wore sensible hats and shoes which today would guarantee people bit parts in any film of that period. The splendid Jowett van of Messrs A. W. Reid Ltd, wholesale tyre factors, was poised on the left for a racing start once the rather large lady had cleared its bows, and both trams and motor vehicles had those narrow slit headlamps designed to protect them at night from the dreaded Hun's aviators. Incidentally, who among the drinking classes remembers McQuat's Ales, served at the Central Market Hotel, marked by the clock on the right?

Eastgate

Before it was opened-up into a striking avenue across the north side of the city centre in the 1930s, what became The Headrow had grown but little in width from the old narrow street divided into the Upperhead and Lowerhead Rows by the Briggate crossing. At its west end, it had connected with Park Lane – and Burley Road which quickly ran out into what was many years ago, little more than a cattle drovers' route coming in from Kirkstall and beyond. At the east end, the Lowerhead Row ended at Vicar Lane and what then became Eastgate tailed off down to somewhat marshy meadows around what is now the bottom of New York Road.

Some 65 years ago, Leeds Corporation bought land in the Eastgate area with a view to extending the city's wholesale and retail markets

northward. But it was not to be and some 25 years later there was a change of mind – by which time the area had reached the stage pictured here, with the Yorkshire Hussar pub in the isolated block on the right. The remaining land in the foreground was sold to a London company on a 125-year lease to construct a block of shops and offices, which would be in keeping with the style of the buildings across the road; thus completing the near-80-year-old dream of some local officials and councillors to have a road 'of outstanding countenance'.

Below the New York Road end of Eastgate, unseen and probably unknown by the millions of people who have travelled over it this past 50 years or so, lies this waterway which, depending on the season, can range from a modest flow to a near-raging torrent. This picture was taken during one of the periodic maintenance jobs. Oddly enough, had it not been for a quirk in a Pennine strata which turned a tiny stream eastward instead of westward, the many problems associated with this run-off might have been those of Bradford's, not Leeds'. Calfhole Beck rises near the crest of Otley Chevin, turns east just above the Shaw Lane area of Guiseley and becomes Shaw Beck. In turn, it becomes Carlton Beck just north of Leeds Bradford International Airport, splits into the Moseley and Marsh Becks, then travels by two routes: one via Horsforth and Hawksworth Woods; the other via Golden Acre Park, Adel, Meanwood and Sheepscar to reach the River Aire. It is the latter which is pictured here near the end of its journey. It has created many problems and over the years attempts to subjugate it have ranged from the primitive to the sophisticated. It has served as an open sewer; it once had powered mills of various types and served as a water source for their boilers; it has also quenched the thirst of steam engines and helped sluice away countless tons of snow shovelled off the city's streets. But like *Old Man River*, it jus' goes rolling along.

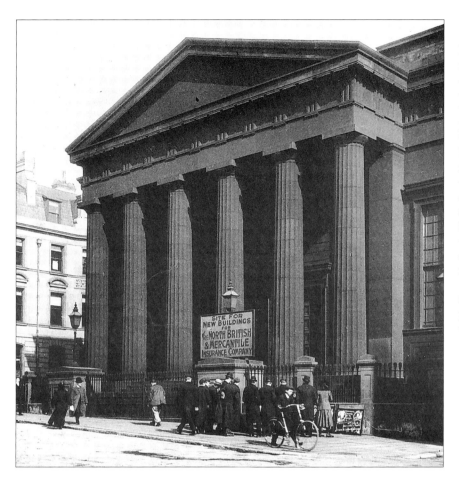

East Parade

Reminiscent of a great structure which once marked the entrance to London's old Euston Station, the East Parade Congregational Chapel – for that is what this is – was a far cry from your average chapel and its Sunday school tea parties. Opened in 1841 this splendid edifice was able to accommodate 1,600 worshippers but neither the principles of its congregation, nor the strength of its hefty pillars was enough to resist an offer which led to its being demolished in 1899 so that the North British and Mercantile Insurance Company could build on the land. What was it, you may wonder, that was causing the business gents and a fashionably-dressed lady to be studying the newspaper contents bills so closely? Surely the *Yorkshire Post* had not already unearthed a South Yorkshire councillor who had got his personal financial affairs mixed with those of the ratepayers?

The Headrow

If there is one name that will be ever associated with The Headrow, and a source of many happy memories for countless thousands of shoppers down the years, it is that of Schofields – a department store par excellence. The frontage of the building stretched almost from Albion Street, to Lands Lane along what was still Upperhead Row in this 1924 view. The Victoria Arcade (through the archway beyond the Cock & Bottle pub with its low gables and large lamps on the left), went through the block to make a left-hand turn to come out in Lands Lane, almost next to the King Charles pub in King Charles Croft. The nameless archway in the centre of the picture was the entrance to Red Hall Court. And thereby hangs a tale – one or two in fact.

It was the ambition of the enterprising Snowden Schofield, who over the years steadily extended his premises on the site, to have the finest department store in Leeds, and this 1988 picture shows what had been achieved over some 70 years. By then the premises covered a vast area but the development had not been without its problems, and one of them took the form of what lay behind the name Red Hall Court mentioned in the previous picture.

And here was the source of those problems – The Red Hall – reputed to be the first house in Leeds built entirely with red bricks. The builder was John Metcalfe, a merchant prince and bailiff of Leeds; and the year was 1628. King Charles I, after his misfortunes in the Civil War, was reportedly held prisoner there after surrendering to the Scots in 1646. At that time, according to an informed article in the then *Yorkshire Evening News* of 18 April 1932, the hall's garden stretched as far south as Albion Place. From there to Boar Lane there was nothing but fields and orchards. As late as the 1840s, poplar trees grew in front of The Red Hall and there was a large garden at the rear where, subsequently, King Charles Croft was established.

The original appearance of the hall held good for many years, but in the years leading up to World War One, Snowden Schofield acquired the mansion

and it was remodelled in 1912 'to meet the needs of Schofield's enterprise'. Care was taken to preserve its historic features but Schofield's expansion (in the 30 years up to 1931 he had moved up from a one-man shop to a business employing nearly 500 assistants), eventually obliterated many of the external features of the hall, resulting in much lively correspondence from members of the architectural fraternity to the editor of the *Yorkshire Evening Post*. In reply, Mr Schofield protested his desire to preserve as much as possible of the hall *within his store:* including the original interior panelling, plus ornately-moulded ceilings and some of the old timbering.

At a later stage, Schofield's store almost surrounded the King Charles pub which stood on the corner of Lands Lane and King Charles Croft. Being within 100 yards of The Headrow it was handy for those walking up there with a thirst. At one time one of the most popular hostelries in Leeds, it was involved in a three-year battle to save it in the early 1970s. The pub got its name as a result of that reported stay at The Red Hall by Charles I. A story has it that John Harrison, the Leeds benefactor who built St John's Church, smuggled a tankard of Leeds ale containing gold coins in to the King.

In more recent years, there was a classic Whitehall boob when Mr Geoffrey Rippon, then Secretary of State, gave planning permission for the Bradford and Bingley Building Society to erect an office block on the site of the King Charles. Meanwhile his civil servants had approved an order making the hotel a protected building! Experts wrangled over the plans: some supported Leeds Corporation's plans to conserve the pub for its 'architectural and historical interest'.

Leeds architect Mr John Tempest claimed that the King Charles building could not be dated earlier than 1840, and had probably been used as a pub only since 1845. Whilst mix-up piled upon mix-up, the regulars continued to quaff their pints whilst the going was good, and members of the Leeds Branch of the National Union of Journalists, who held their monthly meetings at the tavern, were offered the unusual opportunity to spend even more time than usual there, as inspectors, councillors, and consultants came and went and were always good for a pint whilst telling their side of the story.

The shambles ended with a public inquiry before a Government inspector in November 1974, after which it was announced that the pub would be demolished. As a concession, the building society said the building which replaced it would be known as King Charles House.

Our final view of The Headrow takes us back to just how narrow the Lowerhead Row was before being opened-up in the 1930s. Here is its junction with Vicar Lane in November 1929. Lloyds Bank, on the right, is a pretty substantial affair but demolition work – up the Row on the right – is fronted by a sign which heralds the demise of the bank building, however substantial – plus everything else on that side. The sign gives notice of forthcoming road widening and the erection of Lewis's mighty new store (pictured at the bottom of Page 49 in the first edition of *Memory Lane*); which proved to be a triumph of city planning at a time when a world depression might have given the impression that not much could be achieved…

Inner Ring Road

Most long-time 'Loiners' share the opinion that the sequence of demolition, clearance and redevelopment in Leeds has never ceased since the 1950s. Despite a feeling of pride in the general appearance of the city centre in the closing year of the century, there are those who scorn the appearance of some new structures (the Magistrates Courts building at the corner of Westgate and Park Street is Public Irritant No.1), and others regret the demolition of some 'little gems'.

The biggest shake-up of property around the centre came with the clearance of property for the building of the Inner Ring Road from the late 1960s. The area between Meanwood Road and Camp Road was particularly hard hit. This reminiscent of wartime view from Buslingthorpe Lane, shows St Clement's Church, Sheepscar, with debris from the Inner Ring Road workings in the foreground. Ironically, there were those who said that if Leeds had suffered more bombing in World War Two, it would have been redeveloped much more quickly than it turned out …but they were careful not to say that until well after the bombing had ended.

A good impression of how the west end of the city centre looked a quarter of a century ago can be gained from this aerial view of preparatory work for the Inner Ring Road. The new Yorkshire Post Newspapers building is in the bottom right-hand corner, with Wellington Street (and the railway goods yard still in operation to its right), running off towards City Square. The Inner Ring Road flyover had yet to be constructed but 90% of the property in the area bordered by West Street and Wellington Bridge Street (bottom half, centre) had been cleared and preparatory work for the Ring Road's tunnels and approach roads was starting in that area and also beyond the big roundabout which lay between the telephone building on its left and the Brotherton House police offices on the right. For the moment, the new road's progress toward its northern curve stopped just short of the former Leeds Playhouse (near where the cars are parked by the top left side of the picture). And as for parking – even this 1972 shot shows that no sooner was clearance carried-out than motorists moved in: today's clamping mafia would have been sorely tempted to move in after them!

King Edward Street

Now pedestrianised into something akin to the 'Continental look' so desired by some of the city fathers (and mothers, to be politically correct), King Edward Street always had some style; especially when surveyed from the Vicar Lane End so that the sweep of near-matching buildings could be seen up Albion Place, beyond Briggate.

It's metropolitan outlook was no better illustrated than by the King Edward Hotel which had a near look-alike American cousin in downtown Chicago. The Leeds hotel was owned by Matthias Robinson Ltd, and leased to J. Hey & Co., Ltd, the Bradford brewers. It dated back to the reign of the monarch from whom it took its name. In the early 1950s its excellent lunchtime facilities were popular with not exactly overpaid young journalists; who also liked it because there was always the chance of picking-up a good story there, for it was regularly used by stars appearing at Leeds Empire.

The compiler recalls finding the street jammed on one occasion when comedienne Hylda Baker (of "She knows, yer know" fame), pulled-up in an American Chevrolet car almost as long as a Leeds bus and cracked a few jokes with shoppers. At night the King Edward's pop music scene was a big attraction and the racing fraternity also favoured it.

Long-time colleague John Morgan ('Ranger' of *YEP* racing page fame), recalls Harry Higgins, a market trader, telling him that in the 1920s the King Edward's racing clientele included Red Alf, Little Bluey, Big Blue Lightning and Fire-Engine Face. Said Mr Higgins: "I would not be surprised if the tic-tac code was invented in the King Edward. One of my forebears, Mr Guilliver, could neither read nor write but he invented the racecourse signalling which forms the tic-tac code as we know it."

Markets

This picture was taken from a spot where the rear of the Central Market, mentioned earlier, would have been many years ago. It shows the premises of an enterprising company at the east end of the Market Street Arcade which set-up business in 1863, some 40 years after the Central Market was built. But Plants knew a good site when they saw one and they needed no gimmickry or high-faluting television advertising to convince 'Loiners' they sold the right stuff. After all, when they had the time, but were short on money, ordinary folk in the city – and towns throughout West Yorkshire – were adept at hand-picking their own hearthrugs to cover the stone-flagged floors of their cottages and terrace houses; and reight cosy they were. But when there was a bit of spare brass around, it was nice to have one of Plant's specials delivered and be one-up on the neighbours. Plant's sturdy delivery steed, with its own special rug, can just be made out on the left. The buildings on the right appear to be some of the butcher's premises which had surrounded the Central Market.

The granny with the 'gamp', of Giles' cartoon fame in the *Daily Express* (who the author felt was in a picture of the path leading up to Roundhay Park mansion which appeared in the first volume of *Memory Lane*), appears to have shown up again – between the chap in the bowler and the smartly-dressed lady with the white blouse and flying-saucer hat in this early-1900s Leeds Market setting. Take away the names on the splendid stalls and this could be one of the great Gares of Paris; in fact, it is almost the size of the Concourse at New York's Grand Central Station. But don't go round there today expecting to admire that marvellous clock. In due course of time, if you'll pardon the pun, it was moved out to Oakwood and shaken to its foundations several times an hour by clanking trams on their perambulations.

Now here's a treat: some considerable time after writing the caption to the picture of Duncan Street, several pages back, which includes the run-down remains of the Central Market, gutted by fire in June 1895, the author was wading through another section of the thousands of photographs in the *YEP*'s archives when he struck gold: no less than this drawing of the Central Market frontage in all its gracious glory. Drawn by N. Whittock and engraved on steel by J. Shury, it reflects something of the life and times of that popular meeting place.

From left to right: a wagon driver, having delivered his goods, urges his horse out of New Market Street; next – some sort of incident – a small boy with a hoop lies on the cobbles whilst one of three troopers on the causeway holds the jacket of a man whose female companion is being restrained by a second trooper. Next, a lady with a parasol purchases what look like cabbages from the seller with the basket; whilst to the right a boy with badly-worn trousers holds the horse of the gent who has just loaded his purchases into a pannier. The drawing was first published on 15 December 1828.

Park Row

The site of this quite splendid building is well-known to most Leeds citizens and revealing that it was the city's courthouse and prison, opened in Park Row in 1813, will only strengthen the criticisms that thousands of them have levelled at the design of what many refer to as 'The Lego Magistrates Courts building' which was erected not all that long ago at the junction of Westgate and Park Street.

But this 1813 structure had some class, with a portico of four Corinthian columns; the central portion and two wings having panels in bas-relief which contained a fleece – now a portion of the city's coat-of-arms. The building was later used as the General Post Office which, in turn, was replaced in 1901 by the huge white-glazed terracotta-faced offices of the Standard Life Assurance Company. That was later replaced by the 'matchbox on end' Norwich Union Insurance building, demolished with no regrets in 1995 and succeeded in 1998 by the striking nautical look of a building whose transparent ten-storey front entrance and lift shafts are a thing of wonder for small boys.

If the old courthouse stood for law and order at the bottom end of Park Row, the Bank of England building standing four-square at the top gave a distinct impression of stability; and even a friendly domestic touch with its curtained sash windows on the upper floors. The church on the right, which might mystify today's youngsters, was the old St Anne's Cathedral, purchased by Leeds Corporation in 1901 at a cost of £46,000 for road widening. It was replaced by the present cathedral some 100 yards further north and The Headrow was then opened-up on the right for its long, wide march eastward over the hill and down to Eastgate. The original cathedral was completed in September 1838.

Back to the bank: although the building never achieved the fame of its London namesake structure, by being referred to as 'The Old Lady of South Parade' or ditto Park Row, or ditto The Headrow, it had its standards. Today's phone account bank customers will never be tipped a salute by a suitably-dressed doorman, as here; nor perhaps even a second salute from the back-up bobby. Note their shiny footwear; the shiny door handles and kick plates. Those were the days when a clipped "Good morning Sir/Madam – what can we do for you today," was much more appreciated than the eight minutes of Vivaldi or *The Yellow Rose of Texas* which oft-assail the ears in 1999. And, surprise, surprise, you could actually see a real live bank manger: often as cheerful as Captain Mainwaring of *Dad's Army* on his best form…

Park Street

Fortunately for all concerned, Park Street was still two-way when this elegant Fire HQ was purpose-built and the Leeds Fire Brigade moved in there in 1883. With horse power only available, a major turn-out would probably have made a spectacle worthy of any Charlton Heston film; although even then it is doubtful if any chariot race-style turns would have been made into Westgate. And with today's traffic, only a bull-dozer could create that possibility. The new HQ cost £5,000 and included the fire engine house, guard room, stables, an office, blacksmith's and joiner's shop and a tank that held 6,000 gallons of water. The block was swept away for redevelopment in the 1960s and today the Crown Courts building occupies the site – most TV interviews with starring defendants, or more likely their lawyers, take place in Oxford Place, on the other side of the building.

The Queens Hall

For all its claims to be one of the most go-ahead cities in Britain, there is one area in which many business people feel that Leeds has lost-out badly: possibly to the cost of all citizens, shops, stores, hotels, transport development and other businesses of all kinds. A look through the entertainment and what's on pages of the Sunday newspapers in particular gives the clue: at cities – and towns – all over the UK, big concerts and other events drawing large numbers of the public from near and far are being staged at purpose-built concert and convention centres, or refurbished and enlarged existing premises. Mr Gerry Holbrook, then managing director of Yorkshire Post Newspapers, and the author, sat in meetings with executives of

various companies in efforts to get such a scheme off the ground in Leeds. The latter even checked-out various such facilities in the USA – especially where public bonding schemes had provided the cash to set-up highly-successful venues, but it seemed impossible to clear certain political hurdles over here. There has been renewed interest in recent years, and some outdoor events have been very successful; but the city has undoubtedly missed-out on huge revenue-earning events which others have enjoyed for years. Yes, the city did have a stab at it back in the 1960s and 1970s, but the Queens Hall – a converted Victorian tram shed – had limited scope and oft-brought criticism from companies taking part in exhibitions held there.

Perhaps there is some significance in the fact that the letters making-up the rather grandiose title 'Leeds Exhibition Centre' on the left of this picture are only a third of the size of those in the 'Car Park' notice; the latter being the purpose mainly served by the hall in the period after the trams had gone.

The other end of the building, in Swinegate – a dank, often dripping and hardly inviting approach – included the main entrance and the remains of the old Leeds City Transport offices which showed plenty of evidence of deterioration in this early 1980s picture. The then biggest attraction at this venue which had to compete with those in other cities, was a 'Colossal Fleamarket'.

Fortunately, it never descended into running a flea circus, although, as this photograph shows, it did host some full-size circuses: this one being Billy Smart's in December 1961. The steel girders and murky glazed roof of the old tram shed are evident and beyond the bright lights of the circus ring when it got going, the bare and patched-up walls, and the 'facilities' which did anything but enhance the reputation of the city were pretty appalling.

The workmen in the picture were struggling to lay seven tons of coco-matting 'carpet' to give animals, circus staff and performers alike some measure of comfort, said ringmaster Mr Chris Christian who didn't have to trumpet accommodation problems. The elephants did it for him. Now long gone, the Hall will not be missed by most who were ever involved with it: and redevelopment will soon have wiped out all traces. Pity about the trams though: getting rid of them has, perhaps, proved a bigger mistake than not building a Conference Centre.

In recent years we have lived almost continuously with headlines about Mad Cow Disease and its possible effect on humans. Britain's meat industry, at phenomenal cost, has been put under closer inspection than ever before; arguments have raged about conditions at abattoirs, the costly elimination of diseased animals, the need for more meat hygiene inspectors and so on. People here and abroad have been put off, or forced-off – call it what you will – British beef. Politicians who would hardly know a shank from a piece of tripe have given their expert opinions yet despite all, people have continued to eat beef; not a few of them with patriotic motives – or a suspicion of scientists – at the back of their minds. Some of the pictures which follow will, no doubt, raise the question: "How did our forebears survive?" For some, an answer will be the old Yorkshire quotation: "A bit of muck nivver did anybody any harm!"

With the Industrial Revolution set to move into gear, it was not just the manufacturers who saw opportunities in the city's growth. The thousands of workers in clothing factories, engineering workshops and other trades had money to spend and needed to be fed. Enterprising suppliers moved in to meet the need, among them Frederick and Joseph Rinder, cattle dealers and butchers, who brought a large package of land between Briggate and Vicar Lane, roughly around the line of what would become the County Arcade. But first it had to serve their purposes. Slaughter houses were built at the Vicar Lane end and stalls selling provisions set-up nearby; all this between 1814 and 1823. Three years later a bazaar was opened at the Briggate end, almost surrounded by butchers shops whose assistants, if you will pardon the pun, made no bones about dumping butchers' waste into and around the gutter that ran down nearby Cheapside. Meanwhile, upstairs, ladies picked their way through items for sale in the bazaar.

The Shambles

It is almost impossible to imagine that the stretch of fine shops in the County Arcade and the delights of the Mecca Locarno Ballroom (with no less a personage than Sir Jimmy Savile once in charge there) replaced what you see in three of this set of pictures. Unfortunately, the captions with these old prints do not indicate which end is which – Briggate or Vicar Lane – but you quickly get the message. This print of March 1928, shows a boot shop on the left and Cowood & Co., on the right. It appears that someone lived over the shop on the right for the upper windows have a sparkle and they are curtained. But just down that street is a cart with a gory load emerging from the Shambles. With the wind in the wrong direction, the stench at No.12 and adjoining premises must have been awful.

This was the half-decent part of the area, with the shop of T. Whitehouse watch repair specialist, on the right (watches cleaned for one shilling and sixpence, new watch glasses two pence, new watch hands ditto). Someone must have blown the gaff that there was to be a group picture taken because everyone seems to have turned out. And the Midland Railway did not intend to miss a free advert, leaving their giant wicker basket right in front of the camera. Further along there are chopping blocks and sides of beef…

…and further along still there was a bloody trail leading to the central gutter. Dressed meat at a table on the right fronted on to a loading bay where fresh cut joints lay where people walked; three dogs further along licked their lips expectantly as their owners held them in check; at the rear beyond a drain near-blocked by what looks like offal, a large carcass is near-surrounded by pipe and cigarette smoking men and women, some no doubt coughing well on what does not look like the best of mornings.

But wait, assuming you are still with us – it gets worse. Chutes for getting rid of waste material from the upper deck of the slaughter houses protrude into the rain-drenched alley, though no doubt it was welcome. And in the second bay on the right, two well-dressed gents take shelter, their well-polished shoes proclaiming they were a cut above the rest (no pun intended). At which point we end this tour and thankfully draw a veil over what, in all respects, could not have been given a better name – The Shambles.

Even in those days long before hygiene regulations, meat inspectors, or Mad Cow Disease (at least with that name), such conditions could not be allowed to go on; though one might suspect that the close-down of such activity at The Shambles could have been the concern of some who were more worried about their effect on the variety of retail trade outlets in the area, than their effect upon the health of butchers' customers. Towards the end of the century, work started on a dedicated wholesale meat market in New York Street and it opened for business on 24 July 1899. It had all the facilities required to deal in then up-to-date fashion with all aspects of slaughter, plus chill rooms, cold stores, offices and a system of overhead rails which allowed carcasses to be easily moved from one department to another, with little contact with humans or anything else. And its spacious market hall was hailed as a triumph after …well, what else can one say other than simply: The Shambles.

Victoria Square

Still referred to by older citizens as Victoria Square (the good queen's statue was prominently display on a plinth there until it was moved to a controversial site on Woodhouse Moor years ago), the area immediately in front of the Town Hall is now more generally known as The Headrow. The fact is that the 'square' has possibly seen more changes over the years than any other part of the city: and still they go on. Part of this prime piece of real estate almost opposite the Town Hall steps, used to house the Yorkshire Training College of Music (seen here on the left). Later it was divided into offices and shops and in the mid-1980s became the centre of a planning consent refusal row which looked set to its remaining an eyesore for some time to come.

In due course the developers produced amended plans, which satisfied the City Council and the result was the building second from the right in this unusual view through the fish-eye lens of a camera positioned at the top of the Town Hall steps.

Vicar Lane

Everything stops in Wood Street for the photographer: workmen, schoolboys and shoppers obey the request to 'keep still'. The ancient brick-built structure on the right appears to be a stable undergoing some form of restoration on its shored-up wall. But in fact the street, running west from Vicar Lane was being modernised with the laying of a pavement. The 'causeway edges', which seem to have just been delivered from a cart, look good enough to last a thousand years. But it was not to be: within the lifetime of some of those pictured it would become the County Arcade.

Another wall job was going on in Vicar Lane on 13 April 1937. This workman was cementing into position, in the wall of a new building on the lane, the old North Bar stone which was taken from the former building on the site – the old Leeds Workhouse – before it was demolished.

Wellington Street

Today's advertisement hoarding proprietors would give an arm and a leg for opportunities like this: at the turn of the century it seems that if it was empty, and didn't move – stick a bill on it. This was the very east end of Wellington Street around that time and Mrs Elizabeth Cumber's splendid Express Refreshment Rooms would not last for long, nor the three Temperance hotels just beyond them, for this whole block was to be cleared for the creation of City Square. Passengers using the nearby Central, Wellington and New railway stations would, no doubt, miss Mrs Cumber's facilities; except those sitting immediately behind the 'Tea, Coffee and Cocoa' sign, who probably enjoyed more space in a railway carriage.

Westward, along Wellington Street, seemingly decorated for a special occasion in 1897, it looks as if things were approaching the rush hour, according to the position of the sun if not the number of vehicles! Why, there's a chap with a hand cart in the middle of the road actually overtaking a dray. And there was a cheeky wind judging by the way the larger flags are wrapped around their horizontal poles; not least that of John Stockill who kept the Wellington Hotel on the left. Mr Allan Metcalfe, who sent this picture to the *YEP* back in 1986, said Mr Stockill was the father of his wife's aunt, Lena Stockill Watkins, who at that time was still living in Morecambe at the age of 85. In the final years of this block, there were a handful of small shops to the left and the goods offered by the leather shop next door to the pub – trunks and cases – did well for their owner, a Mr Warner, being stacked outside practically opposite the Central Station.

On the Waterfront

It is just possible to read below this view of Leeds that it was engraved by W. Cousen from a drawing by Chas. Cope and published by Robinson and Hernaman, of Leeds, around 1830. The tranquillity of the scene downstream of Leeds Bridge was already being disturbed by the arrival of mills and various works both above and below the Leeds dam, or spillway, in the centre of the picture. Most of the Leeds and Selby Railway, out of sight to the right, was laid and working and sailing barges were busy, with bales of wool well evident. As with all his contemporaries, Mr Cope had not failed to miss Holy Trinity's striking spire (who would dare), but in this case it does seem a trifle exaggerated in terms of height.

The drama of the sky in the previous picture is no less bold in this Chris Lawson shot of a sailing barge at Thwaite Mill, the fastidiously-restored – much of it to working condition – example of what a riverside mill was like in Leeds when waterborne traffic was in its heyday. The barge, named *Jane*, is of 1880 vintage and worked on the Aire & Calder Canal.

Commercial barge traffic, particularly of the coal-carrying variety, was still a regular sight on the Leeds waterfront area until the coming of 'merry-go-round' dedicated coal trains on the railways and the closure of most of Yorkshire's once famous coal mines began to take their toll. This picture was taken in the Dock Basin in August 1969.

And this was the sort of idyllic scene now almost forgotten: a one horse-power barge on the Leeds and Liverpool Canal poses at Redcote Bridge, Armley so that the picture will show its well-decorated stern; the horse that pulled it having been turned around and brought back to face the sun. The barge is well-laden, its cargo hold sheathed with carefully-tucked-in tarpaulin. Just looking at this for a couple of minutes makes one realise what we have lost in terms of serenity and sanity. And has all this rushing around been worth it? Well, you might suppose that Mr Bill Gates has done all right out of it…

The beginning of the shape of things to come for a period could be seen in this 1970s shot of the canal's bridge No.224 at Armley, with debris starting to pile-up on the far bank, and a stone dropped by a young tearaway spoiling the reflection image sought by the chap with the camera.

Almost back to where we were, at Armley – and this time the photographer got his reflection. This cleaned-up section of the canal showed some imaginative painting of the railway bridge structure over the waterway. But in an age where many feel that punishment often fails to meet the crime, or is even meted out, one wonders just how long some of the youngsters at the far side of the bridge will be able to keep their hands off what was once a 'lung' for city centre dwellers.

In November 1975, men who were to install new lock gates behind the Crabtee-Vickers works near Water Lane, in central Leeds, had to empty a section of the canal and this was the sight that met them. Items recovered from the bottom and built into a 'junk mountain' on the bank included oil drums, tyres, bottles, tins, kettles, lumps of iron, wellington boots (but no occupants), bricks, wall-toppings and what-have-you. It had required a massive mechanical dredger to scour the bottom of the canal and then gather-up and remove the mess.

Suburbs Large and Small

Stocks Hill, Armley: and fashions run from the voluminous skirt and shawl of the matronly figure on the extreme right, through the white dress and flower-bedecked hat of the lady passing the baskets for sale at Musgrave's shop; then two girls in formal school attire and a group of younger children looking as if they are on an outing down in the dip. Further along the road there's some demolition going on, and no doubt shouts of "Whoa!" from the chap with the dray horse. Incidentally, nearly all the telegraph poles which appear in these pictures seem taller than they are these days. Had they a choice of taller pines in those days before forests were stripped, or were the wires intended to clear any building in sight?

Here's Armley Town Street on a nice sunny day and you can bet it was a Saturday because there's a free-and-easy feel about most of the activity. The lads playing in the street are well-knickerbockered and shod; the little girl on the right is out to out-do her mother in hat size. There's a young lad in a sailor suit (you could hardly go anywhere in Britain in those days without seeing others like him, Royal Navy attire being to youngsters then, what replica football shirts are to today's soccer fans). And if such patriotism seems curious to some in this laid-back age, note that it was strengthened by the exceedingly tall flagpoles (also noted elsewhere in this book) on four of the buildings in the background: all intended to give prominence to a flag of which practically every UK citizen, city, town and village was proud.

Belle Isle

There are people living north of a line from Seacroft to Horsforth who probably haven't the slightest idea where Belle Isle is located; others think it is somewhere alongside the M1 on the south-east outskirts, others – usually in their 80s – think it used to be in the countryside, south of the city. Well, the last two groups are getting warm in their guessing: Belle Isle was certainly 'way out in the country' when this picture was taken in the early 1900s. It depicts the somewhat run-down building of what was then Dixon's Farm, with walls, windows roof and doors all getting slightly out of true. There were shutters to keep out the winter winds sweeping across from Morley and Middleton; and grandad's rocker against a sheltering wall for summer days. There's a fair amount of livestock but the little girl would be wise to watch that steer with the bull-ring stance. The building was demolished long ago and the farmland covered by part of the Belle Isle estate.

Bramley

Town Street, pictured here in 1906 with all modern amenities creeping in: tram lines and standards, telegraph poles and gas lamps. The position of all the men and the way they are facing indicates that a daily ritual is about to begin: the pub on the left is about to open. A little girl on the extreme right rushes down the slope with her doll's pram, ignoring a white dog which is almost in mid-air as it rushes to greet its compatriot across the street. A grand old chap with a 'full set' beard stands firm, by the telegraph pole, waiting for all the rest to get in t'pub before he makes his entrance. After all, what's the rush – he's been doing it for 60 years or so and nowt's changed. And look at those massive window blinds alongside the well-skirted lady on the right. Yes, the sun really did shine in those days…

Look at a street map of Leeds and left of centre the River Aire makes a large U-shaped bend between Calverley Bridge and Newlay. From the bottom right-hand corner of that bend the ground starts to rise toward Bramley. Had you been going up there in the old days one of the routes you could have taken is pictured here: Rock Lane, at Whitecote, where there was a snug feeling of a little-changed community among the old cottages with their Yorkshire stone roofs, kitchen gardens and occasional outside beams. The fellow balancing the basket was probably delivering freshly-baked bread.

Of course, all life did not begin and end in Bramley, and when the locals felt the urge to travel to foreign parts – like Leeds – they took to one of Isaac Morley's Neat Coaches. This 1805 timetable has a drawing of one, looking a bit like the Deadwood Stage of American musical fame, coming over the hill with a bunch of English theatricals on board. Any reader of this book having problems with present day Leeds bus situations should quote to the driver or operator the last line of Mr Morley's near-200 year old printed undertaking: 'The Proprietor is resolved to spare no expense in order to render Travelling by his Conveyance, Safe, Punctual, and Pleasant,' and ask them if they are likely to be able to give the same undertaking within the next 200 years…?

Bramley AND Leeds.

The Public are respectfully informed that a NEAT COACH will commence on the First of November, from Bramley to Leeds, at the Times mentioned below, viz.:

On Tuesday & Saturday,

To Start from the Cardigan Arms, Bramley,

First Time, at Half-past	8
Second Time at	10
Third Time, at	1
Fourth Time, at Half-past	3

To Return from the Griffin Inn, Leeds,

First Time, at Half-past	9
Second Time at	11
Third Time, at	3
Fourth Time, at	5

And on Monday, Wednesday, Thursday, and Friday,

To Start from the Cardigan Arms, Bramley, at Ten o'Clock in the Morning, and the Griffin Inn, Leeds, at Five in the Evening.

☞ The Proprietor is resolved to spare no Expense in order to render Travelling by his Conveyance, Safe, Punctual, and Pleasant.

ISAAC MORLEY, Proprietor.

ILLINGWORTH AND SON, PRINTERS, BOAR LANE, LEEDS.

1805

Burley

Parts of this view of turn-of-the-century Burley Road, are very familiar to present day morning rush-hour drivers who queue nose-to-tail through this area, down to the Cardigan Road traffic lights, from where they queue yet again toward the city centre. The two houses and shop on the immediate left are long gone, but some of those further along remain. Behind the houses and buildings on the right, the ranks of the Haddons, the Greenhows, the Allertons and others – parallel rows of hundreds of back-to-backs and varied sizes of terraced houses, were so closely packed that some maps had a blank space where they stood because cramming-in all the names would have been impossible. As the years went by, many were demolished and cleared and some of the green of these original outskirts of the city came back; but most of the residents of those friendly old streets were scattered far and wide, often on distant housing estates.

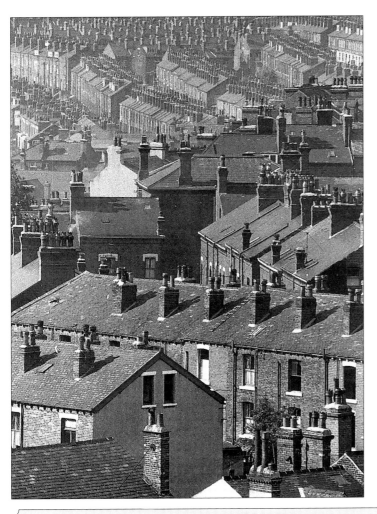

Time was when many southerners thought the whole of the North of England looked like this; and thanks to TV soaps such as *Coronation Street*, there are still those who think that way today. The up and coming generation of children might find it hard to imagine that housing in huge areas of great cities looked like this when coal was king, for practically everyone had coal fires which belched smoke and fumes which Peter Pan and Mary Poppins would have found very off-putting. The Clean Air Act of 1956 put paid to the long-time fogs and smogs which oft-blanketed cities like Leeds and suburbs like Burley, and soot-blackened buildings could eventually be (almost) restored to the colours of their natural brick and stone. Mind you, there are those who swear that the neighbourly spirit of streets like these was often lost for good when people were moved out to huge housing estates in far-flung areas at and beyond city boundaries.

Chapel Allerton

The caption with this picture, taken in 1920, describes it as a view of Stainbeck Lane, near Chapel Allerton. Close examination suggests it could have been the section between Scott Hall Road and Stainbeck Road, near Carrholm Drive.

'Loiners' will find it easier to recognise this location than the one in the previous picture. Yes, it is Harrogate Road at Chapel Allerton, but nearly a century ago. The electric trams had arrived – a driver and conductor are standing on the edge of the right-hand pavement, probably about to swop with another crew – and the size of the flagpoles on buildings on each side of the road indicated a fair degree of patriotism in the area. What looks like the Rolls-Royce of all baby bassinets is parked on the extreme right and the girl across the street is in charge of a smaller model. Oh! for the days when young lasses could walk the streets in peace and a sleeping babe could be left safely on the pavement whilst its mother had a natter with the shopkeeper.

There was a look of a New England church about the spire of the old Chapel Allerton Church in 1909. It had its near-doubles in Vermont and New Hampshire: except that they were built mainly of wood whilst the Chapel Allerton structure was of uncompromising Yorkshire stone.

Cookridge

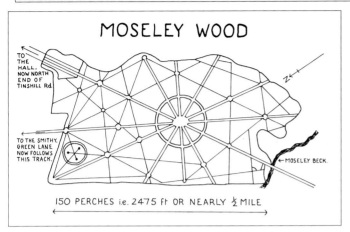

MOSELEY WOOD

TO THE HALL. NOW NORTH END OF TINSHILL Rd.

TO THE SMITHY. GREEN LANE NOW FOLLOWS THIS TRACK.

← MOSELEY BECK.

150 PERCHES i.e. 2475 ft OR NEARLY ½ MILE

Unlike most Leeds suburbs, Cookridge sits outside the natural 'bowl' in which much of the city lies: a feature which shows up more clearly on old hand-drawn maps than it does on many of today's contour maps. The ridge which cuts it off runs in a roughly north-easterly direction through Tinshill (the highest point in the city) which is marked from miles away by its controversial telecommunications tower.

This cutting-off has left Cookridge with a wealth of tree cover and general greenery, making it appealing to bird life in particular and wildlife in general, to the extent that it is not unusual to see foxes trotting along its roads and through its gardens as daylight breaks. Viewed from Scotland Lane, east of Leeds and Bradford International Airport, at the height of summer much of Cookridge is in the rare suburban position of having more trees than rooftops in view.

The plentiful trees are what remains of Moseley Wood, which once stretched along the western edge of the ridge between what is now Otley Old Road and Moseley Beck, which lies in the valley between Cookridge and the airport, alongside the Leeds to Harrogate railway line. The wood has quite a story: Historically, Cookridge harboured a hardy breed of farmers and landowners who built homes to withstand harsh winters. Several farms date back to the 16th century. According to local historian Don Cole, Cookridge got its name not from the long 'hog's back' of high ground, but from an Anglican name, meaning 'Cwica's strip of land'. Anglican settlers are believed to have built huts on former Romano/British sites in the district.

For some 300 years, the cistercian monks of Kirkstall Abbey farmed at Cookridge, following a grant of land to them by William Peynel in 1171AD. Cookridge Grange, a timber-frame building on the site where Cookridge Hall stands, was leased by the monks to Thomas Middleton in 1538. It was extended several times. The decision to rebuild it in the style by which it was known until fairly recently was made in 1753.

Among the structures added in the 19th century was a gatehouse which still stands at the junction of Holt Lane and Otley Old Road. There was also an extension to the 18th-century wall of the kitchen garden which had an unusual feature: this was a brick 'fire wall' which could be heated to protect climbing plants from frost by use of a set of fireplaces, on the back of the wall, that fed heat up diagonal chimneys, thus keeping the wall warm to protect plants on the other side. Conversions and new building at the hall have led to the development of a popular health and fitness club on the site.

Among those who have lived at the hall was a family named Kirke, the most distinguished of them being Thomas, born there in 1650. He had a long list of talents and was a Fellow of the Royal Society. But the achievement which brought him – and Cookridge – international fame was his design for a large geometric pattern of pathways which he had laid down in Moseley Wood.

Topographer Ralph Thoresby's reconstruction of the design, printed here, shows that the pathways covered an area half-a-mile wide and a quarter of a mile deep in the heavily-wooded landscape. By superimposing a modern map over the 1851 six-inch Ordnance Survey, Don Cole was able to deduce that the centre of the 'spider's web' was in the side garden of a bungalow at the corner of Green Lane and Wrenbury Crescent. Such was the fame of the pathways that people came from all over Britain, and as far away as the Continent to walk them.

By the middle of the 20th century, much of Moseley Wood had been cleared and turned over to farming, although there is still plenty of greenery to be seen on the ridge above where these children were enjoying themselves in a pool along the line of Cookridge Beck, or Horsforth Beck as some called it. But these rural pleasures would not last much longer and by the mid-1960s much of this land had been taken up by housing.

Among the houses built in the area when there was still plenty of open space to look over the valley was this one on Tinshill Lane, where Godfrey Talbot, a man whose voice was known to millions through his royal wedding commentaries, and many other broadcasts on the 'wireless', lived for many years.

By a coincidence, another site whose occupants are involved in distributing electronic messages is located in the Tinshill area and has long proved controversial – but never more so than today. Pictured here when it was built at Tinshill top in 1966, it was then known as the Cookridge GPO Tower to most people, as was a smaller tower alongside. At that time the large one had only a few aerials – seen on the left of the third balcony from the top. Today, the whole tower is festooned with aerials of every shape and size. Another, lesser tower across the road on the site of Yorkshire Water's

huge Cookridge water tower is likewise festooned, and what appear to be mobile phone type aerials have appeared on the water tower itself.

Cookridge and Tinshill residents have long been concerned at radio, television and lighting 'blips' in their homes; feeling that the above-mentioned aerials might be the cause. They were also worried, at one time, that the tower might be a hazard to low flying aircraft approaching or leaving the airport (an article written by the author in the *YEP* in the 1960s resulted in a red warning light being installed at the very top of the tower, after a plane seeking to make an emergency landing at the airport was said to have flown too near the tower for comfort).

But at the time of writing, the possibility of a far more hazardous connection with the tower has caused local MP Harold Best to demand a meeting with the National Radiation Protection Board so that it can look into the high number of cancer cases in the area. More women in Cookridge have contracted breast cancer and other tumours since 1989 than in any other area of the city, according to figures from the National Cancer Registry; and local councillor Alan Proctor said that radiation levels around the area where the masts are located needed to be tested for public reassurance.

This picture, taken from the top of the telecommunications tower soon after it was built, shows approximately half of the built-up area of Cookridge (the remainder is off the picture to the left). Practically all the area on which there are houses was at one time part of Moseley Wood. Not long after this picture was taken, the bare fields in the foreground were built on as a part of the Holt Park Estate. Today, Otley Old Road, alongside the fields (and occupied by a solitary Morris Minor when the picture was taken), is a busy morning and evening rush hour artery, serving not only these local areas but points out to Wharfedale and beyond.

Cross Gates

The author's mother-in-law (98 at the time of writing), was born at Chapel Allerton of farming stock who had moved to Leeds from the Ripon area. Her picture appeared on Page 97 of *Memory Lane, Leeds 1* recording the time when she made her first-ever flight at the age of 84. She lived most of her married life in Roundhay, but was pleased to return to the country when her husband retired from his publishing business and they went off to live at Bickerton, on the Wetherby-York road.

However, she still liked to make the occasional shopping foray 'to the city' as she called it, but because she found central Leeds a bit too busy for her taste, settled for shopping in Cross Gates; which was near enough a city after Bickerton. It had a good assortment of shops, and a café which served home-made Yorkshire confectionery which was about as near to her own prize baking products as it was possible to get. Had she been going to Cross Gates 90 years ago, as a little girl, she might well have seen these old cottages in Austhorpe Road, where the picture was taken around 1895.

At some stage or other in later years, she almost certainly travelled along the then built-up Austhorpe Road in the era when this second picture was taken – believed to be between the two World Wars.

Time was, of course, when a chap looking for a place where he could have a quiet read on a summer's day could don his blazer, put on his boater, pop his book under his arm, and stroll along the Cross Gates Bridlepath, with sunshine beckoning beyond the gate.

The chap in the previous picture would have been hard-pressed to carry-out such an idyllic exercise 11 years ago when Peter Thacker's aerial photograph revealed not a single boater, nor a field to sit in, and not even a seat to sit on in the whole of this section of Cross Gates. The Asda store is near the top left-hand corner with Cross Gates Road running across the near-top of the picture. But the memory of that last picture was still retained in the names of Bridle Path Walk and Bridle Path Road, off to the right.

Dewsbury Road

Having worked in London for four years at one stage in his career, and travelled daily from Dulwich Village to the centre, the author has often found similarities between the Old Kent Road and the Dewsbury Road area of Leeds: a finely-mixed spread of housing, shops, cinemas, pubs, small parks, allotments, gasworks and good public transport. There was always plenty going-on: the posters on the wall beyond the New Inn, on the left, show that Tom Mix was starring in *The Best Bad Man* at the Crescent cinema; and the big attraction at the Leeds Hospital Gala at Roundhay Park was to be a Military Display. Further up, a poster for John West's Middle Cut Salmon and a huge blow-up of a portion, served to remind those using the nearby shops that something special was wanted for Sunday's tea…

"Oi! – mind that 'oss," one can imagine the genteel cry of the tram driver as he stamps on his warning bell and winds down the sock-covered handle of his braking device to avoid hitting the back end of the dray protruding over the tram line. The horse and dray are outside the New Inn of earlier days, in this view looking back down Dewsbury Road toward the city. Judging by the position of the sun, it was going home time for local schoolchildren, and friends or older sisters hold the hands of small boys bedecked with large white starched collars as they trot away on the left; the milk float ahead of them being the only traffic to note.

In due course of time, Dewsbury Road, like sections of the Old Kent Road, despite all its attractions and the neighbourly spirit which generally abounded there, was deemed to be in need of a clear-out and redevelopment. Slum clearance, renewal – call it what you will – resulted in huge areas of cleared ground all over south Leeds, interspersed with eyesores like this in the Tunstall Road area, off Dewsbury Road, until the job could be completed. By a coincidence, it was the last few miles of the road all the way from London – the M1 – which finally changed the city end of Dewsbury Road out of all recognition and made it impossible, as many former residents have found, to go back with their grandchildren or great-grandchildren, and say: "That's where we once lived and there were lots of shops, pubs and picture houses within easy walking distance…"

Gledhow

Drivers scooting up and down Gledhow Valley Road catch only a fleeting glimpse of the old Gipton Well, dating back to 1671. A tablet inside the building once stated that it was put up by Edward Waddington. It consists of a hot room with a fireplace, which was roofed-in, and an open-air bath. The Leeds historian Ralph Thoresby described the well as 'a very curious cold spring, which in a Romish Country could not have Miss'd the patronage of some noted saint: tis of late years accommodated with convenient lodgings to sweat the patient after bathing, and is frequented by persons of honor, being reputed little or nothing inferior of St Mongah's.'

Unfortunately, vandals of less honour have attended the protected building several times in more recent years and the curative properties of its waters have done nothing to relieve them of their destructive powers, as shown in this picture taken in the 1980s. What a reflection on the quarter-wits who painted the name 'Harehills' on the roof and wall of a structure which had stood, practically as built for over 300 years, before these unruly disciples of modern-day living set out to underline their limited brain power to all and sundry…

Now for two pictures showing most residents of Harehills in a much better light – in times when folks living there could lead a decent way of life and give consideration to their neighbours; as they did in almost every other suburb in the city. This picture appears to have been taken in Harehills Lane in the early part of this century, and the guess is that it shows either a Sunday School procession or a walk celebrating some special occasion at a local school, for the children are far too grandly dressed for it to have been an ordinary school day.

It reveals some interesting items. From left to right – the taller child holding the little girl's hand on the pavement edge has a hoop slung over his shoulder – an essential outdoor plaything in those days. Outside the shop with the first sunblind on the left, ingenious use has been made of an outsize beer barrel to show off flowers for sale. Alongside it, Mr Parkinson, undertaker and joiner, has an ornate and king-size gas lantern to mark his premises for those seeking his services after dark.

Near the picture's centre is a lad with an early model tricycle and to his right, marked by the bell sign, is a telephone call office. The window of the last shop (No.367 on the right), is filled with dishabilles to delight the ladies although, surprisingly, one of its upstairs curtains is the only one out of trim in the whole row. Perhaps that was the fitting room…!

Harehills

Not far away, in Compton Road, there was a down-to-earth feel among the very precisely laid-out vegetable patches where things seem to have been growing good and strong. A tram awaits the driver's glance at his pocket watch, ready for take-off on the conductor's bell (he must be downstairs because we cannot see him hanging over the upstairs back balcony rail, urging on the tardy schoolboys).

Headingley

There are not exactly enormous numbers of suburbs in British cities whose names are known almost worldwide; but thanks to cricket and Rugby League, Headingley just happens to be one of those which enjoys such a reputation. Strangely enough, before those sports helped to make it famous, it was a massive chunk of ancient timber which put Headingley on the map, and these city-bound tram travellers are just about to pass it on their left. The old four-wheeler has just crested the rise through what has become one of the most notorious bottlenecks in the city. But these passengers had no worries on that score in this 1880s scene, captured by photographer Godfrey Bingley and unearthed at Leeds University nearly a century later; nor were they finicky about their waistlines. 'Nestles Milk The Richest in Cream' proclaims the advert on the bridge of the tram.

That ancient tree trunk which the tram passengers were about to pass was the famed Shire Oak, seen here behind its protective fence in 1908. By then electric trams (although this one is still open-topped) were running between Headingley and Reginald Terrace on Chapeltown Road, via the city centre. Two girls in boaters were cycling past the old Skyrack Inn on the left and the houses across the road looked like they were good for years to come.

…but that wasn't to be, and by March 1968, the shrubbery in front of the Skyrack had been long gone; and so had the houses on the other side of the road. The Skyrack itself remained and is ever popular. But nothing remained in 1968 of the object which had achieved such fame through its being several hundred years older than almost any other object in the area.

A piece of the Shire Oak, preserved at The Original Oak pub (whose sign can be seen at the end of the wall on the right), serves to record that the huge tree went back 'to pre-history.' One story is that it was so big the Romans used it as a signal station. (Would-be bus passengers in today's rush hour melees at that point could probably do with one now). It was later a meeting point for minor chieftains from around the district; and in Saxon times for those who administered the wapentake.

But throughout the 19th century, this grand old tree began to decline, and as it gradually fell away, a decision was made to protect the remaining stump with a fence. Then, on 26 May 1941, the last remains collapsed (many a wag would later say it set the trend for batting by English teams at subsequent Test matches just down the road)!

Tram car No.83 of Leeds City Transport clears smartly away to the right, its conductor having already changed the indicator to Chapeltown in preparation for its return trip. Meanwhile, car No.185 prepares to 'emerge', to quote a favourite BBC word, from Victoria Road, bound for Reginald Terrace, in Chapeltown Road. The powers-that-be at the BBC would, no doubt, flinch at the thought of repeating what it says on the poster on the corner for the Leeds Hippodrome. We have no qualms, for these are the facts of history: G. H. Elliott 'The Chocolate Coloured Coon' was top of the bill at the theatre, singing his then *Top of the Pops* success *Lily of Laguna*. The author's paternal grandmother used to sing it when he was a mere lad, and she could still recall the words before she passed-on in her 100th year; despite having been a Bing Crosby fan in her later years!

It's a pleasant autumn day at the junction of Kirkstall Lane and Cardigan Road, with North Lane going on ahead. Things haven't changed all that much since this – believed to be around the 1920s – picture was taken. The church is still on the left, some of the older cottages up ahead have gone. But just look at that superb lean-to conservatory with the leaded light windows on the right – none of your plastic repros here. And isn't that the maid pulling the curtain aside at the upstairs window, eyeing the photographer? As it is, only a maniac or a very brave chap would try and take a picture from this position today…

One of the more unusual views in Leeds is from Woodhouse Ridge and Batty's Wood, across Meanwood Road to the rising ground beyond. Many people fail to realise just how close Headingley is to Meanwood at that point, and Cumberland Road – not all that far up Headingley Lane from Hyde Park Corner – has this unusual alleyway connecting it with Grosvenor Road, which makes a quick and easy connection with Grove Road and Meanwood. Years ago, it provided a useful shortcut for workers at a mill down by Meanwood Beck; although their passing probably drew a few sniffs from the owners of large properties around the snicket. After someone had gone to all the trouble of providing a stylish archway, what a pity the old gas lamps had to be replaced with concrete lamp standards in the alley which is just over a yard wide in the measurements of its early days…

Pictured in 1894, this imposing structure whose architecture moves inexplicably from the traditional to a touch of Eastern surprise as the eye moves from ground floor to tower has, no doubt, caught the eye of many a test cricketer from foreign fields as they travelled to and from Headingley. Situated to the right of Headingley Lane, when travelling up there from Hyde Park Corner, it began life in 1868 as the Wesley College where Methodist ministers were trained. Having passed its centenary, it was put up for sale in the 1960s and purchased by The Little Sisters of the Poor, who gave it the name 'The College of the Blessed Virgin'. They put it to use mainly for the training of their Junior Professed Sisters, but also allowed the Roman Catholic Diocese of Leeds to use various parts of the building for other purposes. Regular travellers along Headingley Lane will, more recently, have witnessed other changes taking place there, for it is the intention that it be The Leeds Pastoral and Conference Centre, with its attractive landscaped grounds creating a peaceful setting for its well-appointed facilities which well make it a cost-effective venue suitable for a variety of needs.

It took several days of head-scratching at the offices of the Leeds Highways Department and Yorkshire Water to solve the 'where is it?' mystery behind the words printed at the bottom of this picture.

From the start, the author had a hunch about this wide, curving road: everything in the right-hand half of the picture pointed to it being (…) – wait for it! But no local map named a Reservoir Hill, let alone in Headingley; and records scoured by the above-named organisations failed to turn one up. Retired employees also joined the head-scratching, memory-challenged brigade, but without success.

With the picture magnified many times, the author searched for more clues: it was obviously taken before the trams came into use at this well-known location – no lines, no poles, no wires; the wall on the right and the massive gate-posts were, he felt, more than familiar to motorists in morning traffic jams at this point; there was certainly something familiar about the only building – up at the top of the road on the right, but the fall of land in the field on the left was the one doubtful item about it being (…)?

There was nothing to be gained from studying the two ladies in their finery on the seat on the left; or the rude dog behind them doing what a rude dog does on car wheels in a current TV advertisement.

Then, in a conversation about the way the old Leeds Water Authority and later Yorkshire Water had moved a reservoir site, plant and filter beds backwards and forwards from one side of this road to the other over the years – the penny dropped. "I've got it!" cried the author in his best Professor Higgins' style, "It is Otley Road and the picture was taken from its junction with Glen Road! Obviously," he added, "Reservoir Hill never was its official name – the locals simply called it that because of the original reservoir on the right at the top of the hill, and the filter beds later on the left and right which they took to be reservoirs." – End of story!

Holbeck

When the great northern comedians trod the boards at Leeds Empire, those who had long experience knew that introducing local names into their jokes would always give them a stronger appeal. So a 'toff' in a story would be linked with Roundhay, or Adel. Grittier characters hailed from Hunslet, brain surgeons from Gipton Estate.

Holbeck was a name that could be linked to almost any strata of society, for the very sound of it appealed to comedians. Not every resident of West Park or Alwoodley will know that the name comes from the stream that runs through this south of the River Aire suburb: the 'Hol Beck' which, as you might expect, follows the line of Water Lane for some distance through the still busy industrial area.

It was once packed with a wide variety of work places, an important railway engine shed, a mill that looked as if it had been brought from Egypt; another factory with an Italianate tower, plus scores of rows of houses where the workers lived; all of it interlaced with the network of railways – above and around them, laid by several rival companies which had striven to be first to establish a major terminus in the not-so-distant city centre.

As with every other inner city suburb, Holbeck has had its share of what some deem to be '*Coronation Street*-style housing' A real Leeds 'Loiner' might not be too impressed by the description. When, back in 1983, the question gripping Britain was "What is going to happen to *Coronation Street's* Ken and Deirdre Barlow and her lover Mike Baldwin?" the *YEP* sent reporters to Recreation Mount, Holbeck (pictured) to ask families what they thought as 'Street fever' raged nationwide over the soap's crisis. In deepest Holbeck, however, some old Leeds 'Loiners' were not to be used as TV fodder; especially the sort generated in Lancashire. Recalling that day, one of them told the author: "Them Lancashire terraces are nowt like these in Leeds, and that one in *Coronation Street* is just tarted-up for t'programme. There are no breaks in between t'blocks, like ours, for t'lavatories and t'rubbish bins. And these Leeds houses are narrower and taller. Every one has a coal grate leading to its cellar and in t'old days every step and window ledge was scrubbed 'till it shone."

Taken about 1917-18, this picture of the women's annual charabanc trip from the Balloon Inn, Ainsley Street, Holbeck, was sent in to the *YEP* some years ago by Mr Tom Mathers, of Colenso Road, Leeds 11. 'Ainsley Street was known locally as "Mutton Hill" and the charabanc was Benny Wardman's "Little Wonder", wrote Mr Mathers. 'He called it that because it never let him down.' The sidelights were highly-polished paraffin jobs; there was a door to serve each row of seats and the 'chara' was licensed to carry 25 passengers. All the kids in the district arrived to see the trip off, because it was the practice of the passengers to throw pennies into the crowd. On their return, once the ladies had dismounted, the kids got on for a ride back to the garage.

Horsforth

The roots of Horsforth are as well established as those of Leeds, so its townsfolk have never quite considered themselves to be suburban. Their forebears were busy in farming and various other pursuits alongside the Cistercian monks of Kirkstall Abbey. Some local families did very well for themselves in terms of 'brass', a fact underlined by the quite substantial houses in which they lived (see the Low Hall picture in this section).

Among those families were the Longfellows who built a large, though somewhat unusual house at the North End of Long Row in 1640. The long, low structure came complete with its own weaving shed and the family prospered. In due course, however, they decided to try their luck elsewhere and sold up, moving to America where one bright young fellow born into the family at Portland, Maine, in 1807, eventually became internationally famous. He was the poet Henry Wadsworth Longfellow, who was to become Professor of Modern languages and Literature at Harvard University. A small area near the Grey Horse pub in Long Row honours his success. It is named 'Poet's Place.' The Longfellows' original Horsforth house became a pub – The Horse and Jockey, later renamed The Queen's Arms, which still stands.

The area on the right-hand side of this picture, of the lower end of Town Street some 60 years ago, has changed considerably in recent times. Morrison's supermarket stands (out of sight to the right of where photographer took this picture), and there is a comparatively new parade of shops where the car on the right is parked. The Leeds Co-op's sunblinds stand out on the left. The large building at the bottom of the street had various uses: warehouse, café, Salvation Army Citadel, until it fell derelict and was demolished without ceremony in the 1960s, leaving today's open space and 'a road to nowhere'.

Not the brightest of days, but under close examination this shot of Long Row in the early years of this century reveals several items of interest. Firstly, the shop on the left is typical of how they used to be: and some think they might do better if they were still that way! Something of a wonderland for young children, they were crammed with items large, small and curious: deckchairs, washing baskets, feather dusters, baking bowls… you name it, they had it. None of your sanitised no-aroma cellophane-packed everything, with boxes twice as big as the contents. A smart gent with a 'dickie bow', who might have been the proprietor, stands with two assistants on the left. T'lads of the village at the other side. Note the state of the road – it needed a good sweep and it wasn't just the horses to blame. There was a gypsy-style caravan over the wall on the right and in the distance Moseley Wood still held its forest-like grip on Cookridge. Most unusual feature is the goldfish bowl lantern on the gas lamp: a model which graced several local streets.

Today's daily scene of road rage, often brought on by selfish parking on the part of some commuters, it is hard to believe that Station Road could be as quiet as this on an average day at the turn of the century. A nice line in trees on the pavement; no shops on the immediate left; no mini-market further down. And beyond that crazy station bridge at the bottom (see next picture) just look at the wide open spaces leading up to Tinshill – not a shop, house, or pub in sight. No wonder the original Old Ball (even though it did smell of paraffin heaters), and The Queen's Arms (behind the photographer) were so popular.

And here's that notorious bridge: only a nation said to have built its roads over the winding paths where 'one over the top' farmers made their unsteady way home from village pubs could have built such a narrow bridge and S bend; its ends beset by road junctions, curves, exits from the station yard and private premises, and a pavement barely wide enough for two people to pass! But then, the Leeds and Thirsk Railway's builders, faced with everyday scenes like this, were not to know that over a century later their legacy would be a traffic nightmare – for both pedestrians and vehicles. But their pigeon loft-style booking office building, and the snake-like covered staircase to the platform were popular with children. And returning commuters of those days, relieved to get out of the stuffy steam train carriages that brought them up from Leeds, could immediately adjourn to the Fox and Hounds round the corner, followed by an excuse to 'the wife' that 'the train was late again!' In fairness to the L & T, they rarely were…

Many people – including locals – are mystified as to where Brownberrie Avenue got its name. According to local historian and manager of the Horsforth Village Museum, Mr Ron Hartley, it dates back to local worthy William Stanhope, who was the Tax Collector for Yorkshire, said to 'enjoy his port and pudding'. So much so that when he began to suffer from gout and stomach upsets he pricked-up his ears at local stories that a brew similar to senna, made from the pods of wild broom which was plentiful in the rough land around Horsforth and Cookridge in those days, was beneficial to those suffering such complaints. William tried it out, found that it worked, and was so taken that he decided to name his house 'The Brownberries', having consistently mis-pronounced the real name of 'broom' berries. The house still stands – directly opposite the entrance to Trinity and All Saints College. However, its name was changed to 'Brownberrie Manor' by a later resident, a Mr Catton who was in the engineering business in Leeds.

Another of the Stanhope clan (their name is perpetuated by a local hotel), was John, a yeoman farmer who, following the dissolution of the monasteries, bought Low Hall, on the Calverley side of Horsforth in 1568, and it remained in the family for some 200 years. Within blessed memory it became a well-known restaurant which attracted customers from over a wide area. Its massive old beams and equally reassuring stonework in the upstairs Calverley Room (pictured) was complimented by fine woodwork and decor in the large ground floor restaurant. Its food and facilities brought many compliments from, in particular, personnel of international airlines and travel organisations who held various functions there. It is still praised by the chief executive, in Sydney, of a top Far East airline. But then, he once lived in Roundhay. Sadly, the restaurant closed some years ago when the Hall was sold for other use.

Hunslet

It seems an odd coincidence that the face of Hunslet, an area which was the cradle of much of the industrial activity that helped build Leeds into the great city it is today – especially when so much of that industry was devoted to transport – has been split-up, torn apart, rebuilt and then changed all over again by the development of transport links into and out of the city.

A form of railway ran through Hunslet long before the later world-famous Stockton and Darlington and Liverpool and Manchester railways came into being. An Act of Parliament of 1758 authorised the building of a waggonway between the Manor of Middleton 'to supply the inhabitants of Leeds with coals for their use and consumption'.

Charles Brandling's double-track line from Middleton to Casson Close, near Leeds Bridge, where coal staithes were located, established a record as a pioneer line built to a gauge of 4ft 1ins which was converted to standard gauge in 1881. It established another record on 20 June 1960, when the Middleton Railway Preservation Society ran its first a train over the line making it the first standard gauge line to be successfully preserved by amateurs.

Brandling's efforts concentrated on coal traffic; the Midland Railway had goods and passenger traffic in mind when it drove its main line through Hunslet, and in the race to be first with a major station in the city centre, was arguably the winner – although the Midland Station was still south of the River Aire, near Hunslet Lane.

The Midland's main line, much of it in a broad cutting with four lines, cut through Hunslet and it can be seen here – a black swathe – running up from the bottom right-hand corner, then cutting across Holbeck where the later London Midland and Scottish had a mainline engine shed, before curving round to enter City Station.

Almost halfway up the right-hand side of the picture, a straight line of four tracks cuts off from the curve and goes ahead into the huge Hunslet Lane Goods Yard, where nearly 30 tracks can be seen fanning-out from the entry lines just beyond the two gas-holders. Eventually, all that site was cleared and is today the location of the Crown Point retail park.

In due course the coming of the M1 divided Hunslet up yet again – it, too, can be seen here coming in from the bottom right-hand corner and heading for the city centre up, over, under and around cleared demolition areas and existing roads, a short time before it was officially opened; and long before the M621 and other sections of highway infrastructure were built.

The faces of that part of Hunslet and the bottom end of Dewsbury Road would never look the same again, and even old-timers find it hard to spot where they used to live and/or work: sometimes because such structures and even the ground they stood on has just plain disappeared! Leeds station is still identifiable at the top centre of the picture, with the Hilton National Leeds City hotel rising alongside the Dark Arches.

There's just a whiff of the Continent (as we used to know it) in this drawing of Hunslet in the early 1800s. Folks in their finery, market stalls and structures that would do credit to some French region; a church with a Flemish look, swings and er …what's this: you would hardly find a stage set-up with the name O'Brian's on it in the Moselle – and that Punch and Judy show on the extreme right is truly British. Yes, it was Hunslet Feast. But it couldn't all last – the Hunslet Old Chapel was demolished in 1862.

There are some fascinating – and quite old – structures on the left of this undated photograph, said to be Hunslet Lane; although the street sign 'Coal Staith Road' just beneath the roof line of the building on the left, would indicate it wasn't a million miles from the Leeds Bridge end of Hunslet where there were coal staiths. The tram lines had certainly arrived and other signs of progress include the well-polished lantern of the gas lamp, and indications that a third storey had been added to the premises with the row of shops.

Although Hunslet had a worldwide reputation for fine machinery produced in its many engineering works, it had no history of fine boat building and this odd craft, braving the elements of Hunslet Lake in 1907, bears that out: if the somewhat apprehensive expressions of the passengers are anything to go by. The vessel had such a 'built in a garden shed' look about it that, complete with dog, it only needed Charlie Chaplin to come along and the farce would have been complete. Mind you, that pavilion in the background would have done credit to some of today's city parks, where despite some valiant efforts, facilities are generally less grand than in days of yore…

In the years post-World War Two, vast swathes of Hunslet were reduced to rubble in the process of slum clearance and the demolition of old factory buildings. At times there was little difference between these areas and districts in other northern cities which had suffered more from Luftwaffe bombing than had Leeds. This view was looking toward the city centre from the wasteland around Hunslet Hall Road in 1973.

Time was when a score of factory chimneys on this skyline belched smoke which blackened the buildings of Leeds. By December 1987, only three remained and of those only one was smoking. The skeletons of the big factories they had served are gaunt and silent. In the foreground nature had begun to reoccupy just one corner of the huge Hunslet Goods Yard (indicated in the aerial picture at the start of this section) which had closed in January 1972. Night and day, there was just the wind sighing through the tall grass and branches where, years ago, the chimneys of scores of shunting and main-line goods engines barked day and night. Buffers clanked, whistles blew and (claim some old railway hands), the ghostly crew of one loco have occasionally been seen, apparently reporting for duty. True or false? There would certainly be little for them to do today for the big Crown Point Retail Park, opened in September 1989, now covers all this site.

At the time of writing, the future of Hunslet Mills, in Goodman Street, a steam-powered flax-spinning mill built in 1838-40 beside the River Aire, was anything but certain. The buildings are a monument to the times when parts of south Leeds rumbled, trembled and vibrated to the workings of industries which had helped turn Britain, and particularly England, from a rural economy into a world power.

Machinery and products made hereabouts were exported all over the world, and the quality was such that some of it can be seen still in use in places as far apart as India, South America and South Africa. But what was learned, then taught, eventually rebounded as the original machinery we had exported was copied, developed and in some cases became more advanced than our own and that fact – coupled to lower wages at those points overseas – helped turn sections of industrial suburbs such as Hunslet into near-industrial ghost towns.

Following some controversy, its windowless main structure gazing across the river to the Cross Green industrial estate, the long-empty Hunslet Mills was declared a Grade II* listed building and is now the subject of on-going negotiations. Meanwhile, it cannot be demolished; so it might just face a useful future as per the example of the Sugerwell tannery premises described in the Meanwood section of this book.

The Cuckoo Steps, off Pepper Road, led over the railway near the old rugby ground, not all that far from Middleton Colliery, wrote Councillor Len Hodgson, of Leeds, in a 1985 letter to the *YEP*. 'As children we often visited this area which formed a part of our weekly afternoon walk following Sunday School, but on Mondays that quiet atmosphere changed from tranquility to the bustle of industry and from 7.00 to 7.30am there was a series of works' hooters blowing, with the men hurrying up Pepper Road to clock in.

'At 5.00pm, droves of men would leave their engineering works and fill the pavements as they made their way home from the factories where they made Leeds a great engineering city.'

The author recalls, in the early 1950s, Mr Hartley Shawcross, the then editor of the old *Yorkshire Evening News*, asking him to write "a funny piece to go on the front page every night". Explained the canny editor: "When fellows have been in a thundering machine shop hot as an oven all day; then come out into the sleet to battle their way on to steamed-up, clanking trams, I want them to read something that will give them a lift and a laugh." It worked – and became popular. Would that his advice was still acted upon on some of our national, politically-strewn front pages…

Hunslet Boys Club

No reference to Hunslet in a publication of this type would be complete without mention of the Hunslet Boys Club: an organisation born of conditions in an industrial suburb which took hold, then grew into what has often been held up as a national example of how to encourage young men to give of their best.

On 14 March 1973, the *Yorkshire Evening Post* paid particular tribute to a man who had turned a wartime club for ARP (Air Raid Precautions) messenger boys into one of the best youth centres in the north. He was Clifford Goodyear, JP, MBE, whose awards resulted from a life's work of selfless dedication from which he was then retiring at the age of 65.

Hunslet Boys Club was founded in 1940 by Dr John Wyllie for lads who had helped to form a 'messenger corps' after Hitler's bombers had knocked-out several ARP posts in the area. As more boys volunteered for duty, the club was moved to a former Wesleyan Sunday School in Waterloo Lane.

Growth continued after the war and in May 1971, the Duchess of Kent opened the club's splendid new £100,000 premises in Hilledge Road and Cliff Goodyear's world was near-complete.

In later years, grandfathers who had been original members helped out with their sons and grandsons, and this unbroken line of succession was one of the club's great strengths. The Hunslet boys (ages 11 to 21), acquired from the outset a powerful feeling of really belonging; so that they went out in to the world with a strong will to serve others.

The club's wide range of activities – particularly sporting – led to national recognition and honours. It's fund-raising and charitable activities raised large amounts for all manner of causes. A pair of boxing gloves, signed by Mohammed Ali and Henry Cooper, were willingly sent to the club so that they could be auctioned to raise funds.

Members learned skills in various crafts; they grew up to take responsible jobs (at one time the ranks of the local police force included ex-members running into double figures); others went on to take senior posts in other boys clubs and one of them became National Secretary of the National Association of Boys Clubs.

But the going was not always smooth: at one stage party politics on Leeds City Council looked set to interfere with the running of the club through the threat of the withdrawal of financial support, but the hitch only strengthened the members' will to raise funds.

In March 1973, Cliff Goodyear retired and was given a magnificent send-off. He had seen good in the city's youth despite many examples of waywardness. "It's the circumstances they find themselves in that turns them into tearaways. So often they get their lead from adults," he said, adding: "give youngsters the right environment and a good example and they'll respond all right."

With the club gone from the empty ex-Sunday School premises where it all started, the building became the target of other youngsters who clearly fell into the tearaway category: the bottom picture here shows the exterior of the premises in Waterloo Road; the top one shows the interior after the vandals had done their worst. In the end, local residents petitioned the city council for the building to be demolished.

But for older people in Hunslet, nothing can erase the memory of the good times – and good deeds – which resulted on those premises: because some people took the trouble to care.

Hyde Park

Possibly as stylish as its London counterpart in the days when parks were respectable, well-kept areas where ladies and gentlemen could take a pleasant stroll, and children could play in safety, the stretch of ground that bears the name Hyde Park in Leeds is, all too often these days, more generally known as Woodhouse Moor. Yet the crossing where the Woodhouse and Headingley Lanes, and Woodhouse Street and Hyde Park Road converge, is more often than not called Hyde Park Corner.

No dates appear on the first two pictures of this location, but the general opinion is that this is the oldest. Looking up Headingley Lane, from which a Chapeltown-bound tram is emerging, it shows a fairly old cottage and shop property on the corner of Hyde Park Road on the left. To the right, set back from Woodhouse Street, are the premises of Tebbs, dyers and cleaners. An early example of careless driving on the left has a horse and carriage cutting the corner into Hyde Park Road, although the person halted in her crossing was probably too much of a lady to develop road rage...

If the sequence is correct, by the time this picture was taken Tebbs had gone, and their premises taken over by Johnsons The Dyers (Established 1817). Mould's Hyde Park Hotel loomed massively on the Woodhouse Street corner and on the left the well-known names of Maypole and Lipton graced the shops fronting a large building which had replaced the cottages. Some mother had no qualms about leaving her baby in its pram outside Lipton's where the local milkman had left his served-straight-from-the-churn device at the pavement edge. Meanwhile, another wrong-side merchant with a horse and trap confuses a pedestrian in the foreground and a cart being pushed into Woodhouse Street is also on its wrong side. Was there an American influence from the nearby university that affected all these road users?

By September 1983, all the drivers and riders in the vicinity had got it correct, thanks to some distinctive road markings and traffic lights. The mock Tudor of The Hyde Park hotel, with its reassuring Tetley Ales sign indicated that changes come and changes go, but if you're directing someone from the city centre to Headingley Cricket Ground, use the Hyde Park pub as a point of reference…

Killingbeck

One of the oldest houses in Leeds, this substantial medieval farmhouse, known as Wyke Bridge Farm, was occupied by a family named Thompson whose name appeared in the Whitkirk registers as early as 1638. Evidence of their occupation included the letters 'W.T.' carved over the parlour door and were probably those of Walter Thompson, whose named appeared in the Hearth Tax Roll of Charles II, under Seacroft Township.

The building was also mentioned in the Whitkirk Church burial register of 1697 in an entry referring to Elizabeth Thompson of Wikebridge. Note that the spelling varied over the years. Its name, it seems, came from the beck (latterly known as White Beck) which ran down from beneath the old York Road, and the house stood between the line of what became the 'reserved' tram track, and the London North Eastern Railway (LNER) embankment, not far from the junction of Selby Road and the present York Road.

In 1924, the farm buildings were purchased from Lord Halifax by Leeds Corporation, and some were demolished to allow the widening and diversion of the York Road. The main house, however, was occupied until at least the late 1930s. In 1945, the Inspector of Ancient Monuments to the Ministry of Works announced it was likely to be preserved; noting that a heraldic plaque, believed to be of 15th-century origin over the 17th-century fireplace, was of particular interest.

In 1946, there was a plan for the building to be renovated at a cost of £1,500, if the Leeds Corporation Finance Committee would agree the expenditure. However, this idea fell through and in February 1948, it was announced that the house would be taken down piece-by-piece, and then rebuilt, possibly near Kirkstall Abbey, to be exalted as the only remaining truly Tudor building in the city.

Certainly, the building was demolished, but what happened to it then is something of a mystery: does this gem remain in some Corporation store, its many pieces carefully docketed, awaiting its rediscovery? Or has it gone forever or, perhaps, been used as fill under the M621?

Back in 1971, Mr C. M. Mitchell, the then Leeds Museums Director, was buttonholed by a *YEP* journalist, but could offer no explanation: "I only came here in 1953," he said, "so I cannot be blamed for the disappearance."

Later, after some head-scratching, and perhaps with the thought that the ghost of the departed Elizabeth Thompson of Wikebridge might haunt him for life, he recalled that once, when seeking some items to furnish the famous replica old street at Abbey House Museum, some panelling from the stores was used in the street's old watchmaker's shop; and two inglenook seats went into the pub. He also recalled that yes, the old coat-of-arms from Wyke Bridge Farm was in the store …but there was no trace of the rest.

So, if you happen to be motoring along the York Road one dark and foggy night, and a ghostly maid in rural attire stops you and says she's dying for a sit down …be a good citizen. Give her a lift to Kirkstall.

Kirkstall Road

It's a better than evens chance that somewhere around Leeds today are some lads who were present when this picture of Standard VII was taken at St Simon's School, Ventnor Street, Kirkstall Road, in 1932. The photograph was sent to the *YEP* for use in the Old Yorkshire Diary in April 1987, by Mr Jack Hird, then living at Dudley Walk, Lead Lane, Ripon, who is on the extreme left in the back row.

Mr Hird recalled that most of them lived in the 'Alphabet Streets' where deprivation was widespread. The teacher on the left was a Mr Hodgson, a stern disciplinarian who had an eye for playground cleanliness. The teacher on the right was Mr Marshall, a kindly-mannered man who later went on to Burley National School.

As with many such pictures of that era, just about all of these pupils would be eligible for call-up in World War Two and Mr Hird knew several who made the supreme sacrifice. Despite all, he had many happy memories of those days living off Kirkstall Road.

Not exactly a sight to set a dog's tail wagging with delight – the soot-blackened old RSPCA premises on the south side of Kirkstall Road backed on to a chemical complex that produced assorted whiffs not exactly guaranteed to tempt canines into a long stay. Short of the Victoria Hall roof at the Town Hall before it was cleaned-up, few buildings in Leeds could have gained a much more melancholy appearance than this one, thanks to years of pollution. What a pity some (pardon the pun) wag didn't see fit to replace the letter P on the No Parking signs with a letter B…

The Leylands

At the time the compiler was selecting these pictures from the *YEP* archives, some heat was being generated in certain northern quarters regarding immigrants/refugees who, it was alleged, were to be moved from the south of England to Leeds, and other northern cities, because local authorities down south were finding the financial pressures of the situation almost overwhelming.

Pointing-out how Leeds had welcomed such people in the past, a City Council spokesperson cited a list of nationalities and, in particular mentioned people of Polish and Jewish extraction. What this person did not qualify was that most of the Poles had fought on the Allied side in World War Two and were unable to return to their homeland afterwards; or that the large influx of poor Jewish immigrants of an earlier era had fled Russian pogroms.

It might also have been worth stating that the majority in both groups, starting almost from scratch, were independent and worked hard and diligently to improve their situations. Many went on to make significant contributions to the industrial and commercial success of Leeds in very tough times, when welfare benefits for people such as them were either non-existent or certainly not what they are today. The poorer Jewish refugees settled mainly in an area known generally as 'The Leylands' and here is a group of their children in Bell Street in 1899.

Adept at tailoring, the Jews quickly realised the opportunities that existed in an area with the best cloth-making mills in Britain around its fringe. Some of their workplaces grew, literally, from enterprises in upstairs rooms in their tiny, crammed homes, to factories which became nationally, and even world-famous. Such was the scale of growth that various branches of the trade union movement became involved in the tailoring business and the Jewish Tailors, Machinists and Pressers Trade Union was established in 1893 and erected this trades hall in Cross Stamford Street in 1910.

Slum clearance schemes began to change the face of the areas where the original Jewish refugees had settled – around the north end of Vicar Lane, North Street (where one small, green inner city patch was best-known locally as the 'Jews Park') and also around Mabgate and Sheepscar Street. But those who had worked to put themselves in better circumstances had already moved out of 'the ghetto', as the Leylands area was known to some, and started a progress that took succeeding generations to homes up through Chapeltown, Potternewton and Spencer Place to Moortown; Moor Allerton and Roundhay; then to Alwoodley, Wigton Lane and beyond. Behind them, houses under threat from clearance – houses where their parents and grandparents had worked all hours in attic workshops, were quickly ransacked and wrecked by vandals and vagabonds. Only the ghosts of un-Yorkshire accents and music, and memories of harsh Eastern European treatment remained; as in this crumbling wreck of one of the last of The Leylands.

Meanwood

That tinkling beck, described elsewhere in this volume, which starts out near Otley Chevin, and by diverse routes becomes Meanwood Beck during its journey to join the River Aire, is not the only water source of interest in the suburb. This curious structure on the left, looking like the sort of kennel a guard dog would occupy at a border crossing, is the historic Revolution Well. An inscription on its side reads:

> Bog in the adjoining field drain'd,
> Spring open'd, and conducted hither,
> For the benefit of the pafsenger, and the neighbouring houfe,
> Novr 5th. 1788.
> the 100th Anniverfary from the Landg of King William,
> in memory of which happy Era this is, by Jofeph Oates,
> Infcrib'd the Revolution Well.

The well is on the left-hand side of Stonegate Road (when going up), almost opposite Carr Manor, and was originally at the head of a small stream; but was moved slightly some 60 years ago. According to a *History of Meanwood* by Arthur Hopwood, Joseph Oates lived from 1743-1824.

Getting back to Meanwood Beck; a million miles from today's traffic-swirling morass in and around Meanwood's centre, this delightful study of the beck wandering through the wood on a balmy Victorian summer's day in 1887, was captured by Leeds amateur photographer Godfrey Bingley. His pictures had a quality and balance that some of today's professionals would find hard to beat.

Twenty-three years after Geoffrey Bingley's picture was taken, an unknown photographer captured this charming study of a young girl whose dress and demeanour is rarely to be found today, other than in top-ranking 'period' films or TV series. The picture was taken on the path through the woods between The Hollies and Hustler's Row. Four years later, in woods in France, a war would erupt that destroyed countless trees in other pleasant spots and the world would never be quite the same again…

More destruction – and this in the heart of Meanwood. In an age when people could roam around Leeds and its suburbs at night, on foot, on trams and buses, without any concerns whatsoever; there were those of us who took a tram out to Meanwood for a night at the Capitol ballroom. There was a cinema, too, of the same name. But if you were full of jive, jitterbugging, bobby socks, zoot suits, 'brothel creeper' shoes (the latter name a left-over bit of army slang from World War Two, not a reflection on Meanwood's younger set), then the Capitol was the place to be. But like all good things it had to come to an end and after a spell as the Cat's Whiskers nightclub (where the 'cage' in the foreground of this picture formed a curious part of the entertainment), it was demolished, leaving the sound of the hits of Glenn Miller, Harry James, Count Basie et al to waft up, up and away into the night sky over Woodhouse Ridge…

When they built factories in the north of England, they didn't mess about. In the old days when you rode by train through the mill towns and the industrial areas of cities like Leeds, there was 'summat solid' and interesting to look at: unlike today when there is a similar look about every town you go through with their ranks of aluminium-clad aircraft-hangar-style warehouses etc, and Salford Quays' style of red-brick office blocks sporting chunks of 'what is it?' statuary at their front doors.

The disturbing thought is that when the bad times hit the textile and engineering trades years ago, it took a long time to clear the machinery etc, and even longer to remove the structures. Today, having pulled all the plugs connecting plastic boxes to a power supply, it is possible to have everything and everybody out in a week-end, leaving only a thin shell of a building as a statement of the 'modern' Britain favoured by some politicians.

Not so, when Sugarwell Works were closed in Meanwood Road. A classic example of a production establishment created by people with both feet on the ground, the massive former tannery – a Grade 2 listed building – resisted the worst efforts of the vandals and survived years of dereliction to reach a point where its possibilities attracted attention from developers. So, as this is being written, the four-square old building is set to have a new lease of life, providing apartments and other facilities which will include old cottages and the mill race building in addition to the main tannery building's development.

Middleton

Famous for its pit and more recently its preserved railway, going back much further in time Middleton was also well-known for the windmill which could be seen from afar on this lofty point of south Leeds. Although originally a substantial structure, it quickly became derelict in the years following its retirement and was declared unsafe and demolished in 1941. An old Middleton resident recalls grandads taking grandchildren to see 'the crocodile climbing-up the side of the windmill,' leading to screams and little legs carrying their owners off in all directions. The object was, he says, just a part of the mill's machinery.

Moortown

No Marks and Sparks, no take-aways, no traffic lights, roundabouts, Ring Road or Fire Station. But there was a Post Office and telegraph office at Moortown in the early 1900s. On a quiet news day you can imagine a *YEP* reporter and photographer being sent out there with instructions to 'see if you can find something interesting'; and an hour after arrival, being tempted to scribble a note, reading: 'We are being attacked by 600 Apaches…' then asking the startled telegraph operator to wire it to the news desk…

Oakwood

Even if they did not know it before, readers who have noted the Markets section in this volume will now be aware that the imposing clock tower which used to stand in Leeds City markets was moved to Oakwood and installed on an outdoor location in the early 1900s. However, it will be doubtful if many 'Loiners' born after 1930 will recall this rather striking building which, for over 60 years, stood on a site within about 100 yards of where the clock still presides over the Wetherby Road, Roundhay Road, Gledhow Lane and Oakwood Lane junctions.

Known as the Roundhay Park Entry Lodge Complex, it was on the curve between Princes Avenue, which crosses the Military Field (better known as Soldiers' Field) and Wetherby Road. The plot of which it was part was bought for £20,000 and included Hartley's Farm, five Horseshoe Cottages, the smithy and the residence of Joseph Hobson with its outbuildings and gardens.

The Italian-style building was erected in 1872 and used mainly as offices for the Parks Department staff. A police station was established there in 1914.

The Roundhay Park estate itself was purchased by John Barran at auction in 1871. In turn, he sold it to Leeds City Council under the Act of Improvement of 1872. The Manor and Lordship of Roundhay and Seacroft was bought at the same auction by John Sagar-Musgrave, of nearby Red Hall.

On 21 July 1923, the tramway from Oakwood to the Canal Gardens, Roundhay Park, was opened and here's tram No.48, as polished as the product advertised on its rear balcony. The west end of the Entry Lodge complex looms over the scene as the tram crew climb aboard for what many remember as the rocking and rolling crossing of Soldiers' Field

via the reserved track (a blessing for the crew, who would thus avoid the slipstream aroma from the midden cart going up ahead of them).

It seems a shame that this imposing building was demolished, following agreement in Leeds City Council in January 1937, for it made an imposing sight on the approach to what was, for many years, one of Britain's finest city parks and was a source of pride to Leeds citizens of every calling, whatever suburb they hailed from. Regretfully, it does not appear to enjoy quite the same reputation among some today, although it is a great asset to the city.

Whitkirk

A preservation order on the grounds of historical or architectural interest makes this house in Selby Road, Whitkirk, part of Leeds Heritage. Prominent between the upstairs windows is a Knights Templar cross with the date 1744. Before alterations around Vicar Lane and Lower Headrow in the city centre, described and illustrated in *Memory Lane, Leeds 1*; there were several homes in that part of Leeds with similar crosses.

They are a survival of the days when citizens were obliged to have their corn ground at the King's Mill, Swinegate (on the site of the old tram sheds). Those who could lawfully sport the Knights Templar cross were exempt from this ruling. Edward Hudson, of Roundhay, purchased the rights to the King's Mill and its soke (levy) for £32,000 in 1815. Twenty-four years later, Leeds Corporation bought-out the monopoly for £13,000, thus removing this burden from its citizens.

The house to the right of the one in the last picture stands on the corner of the Selby and Colton roads at Whitkirk, with the parish church of St Mary's in the background. On the wall of this second house which faces the church, there is a similar Knights Templar cross, but the accompanying date is 1732. The church itself is mostly 15th century, with stone pillar bases of an earlier 12th-century building.

A sad sight opposite St Mary's in January 1973, were the remains of this 200-year-old barn which had been allowed to become derelict. It is hard to understand why no preservation order covered this structure whose 2ft thick walls would, with some reasonable care, have carried it well into the next millennium. As it is, much of its massive stonework seems to have 'walked', leaving it with a Flanders 1915 look about it…

Whoever commissioned the message on this headstone, which is possibly more than 200 years old, in St Mary's churchyard will no doubt be regarded by many folks today as having been ahead of his time. Or does it justify a belief that nothing changes? It reads: 'This world's a city, full of crooked streets. Death is the market place where all men meet, if life was merchandise that men could buy, the rich would always live and the poor die.'

Woodhouse

Anyone raised in Woodhouse in the era of trams, back-to-backs, seemingly endless terraces, cobbled streets and gas lamps, might find it difficult to conjure-up a vision of anything remotely like a farmhouse in this near-inner city suburb. The fact remains that it has been suggested that's what this old place in Woodhouse Street could have been.

The photograph was taken in the 1890s when, (apart from the remodelled chimney stacks), it was possibly up to 300 years old; especially when the style of gable on the wing on the left is considered. The stonework in the yard is believed to have been the site of a well, or hand pump (which might have saved the old lady on the left from having to trail round the corner with her bucket, had it survived).

But consider – the stonework as a whole was truly massive. Could the part on the right have been an inn? There's an unreadable sign on the extreme right and there's something like the back of a tap room settle to be seen through the window…

The old saw about a chap asking directions of a puzzled old rustic and getting the answer: "If I'd been thee, I wouldn't have started from 'ere," comes to mind when looking at this structure – and there are many equally curious houses perched on minute pieces of level ground clinging to hillsides throughout West Yorkshire. One imagines that few builders of today would choose to tackle such a site. The location is Johnston Street, Woodhouse, where life for the residents over the years must have been full of ups and downs…

Even university students of (many) a yesteryear would be hard-pressed to recall this view of Woodhouse Lane. Tram No.277 is heading for Victoria Road, Headingley, whilst No.204 is coming down the hill, city bound and about to overtake the inevitable railway dray; which was the fore-runner of today's inevitable 'white vans.' Two postmen wearing those caps of the day which made them look like border guards in some Alpine state, chat at the entrance to Blackman Lane, on the right, and flat caps predominate among the males in view.

Strangers to the city reaching this point have been known to say: "Oh! Look – a church with a spire at each end"; the optical illusion created by the fact that one church is just behind the other; but a second glance reveals the spires are quite different. But what's missing? Well, there is no optical illusion about the fact that the Parkinson building, and its famous tower, is not there.

The great white building, first mooted in the 1920s, was not completed in all its glory until 1950; various hold-ups – not least World War Two – slowed progress.

Woodhouse Moor, 1897. Not the best of days, but how refreshing to see pristine paths and seats; no litter; gloriously decorated archways; bandstand, fountain with statue; clock tower with drinking fountain and some charming lanterns and …er, what's this? Gad! Sir, there's a weathervane cut to the shape of a fox – right here virtually at the city's gates. Perhaps that old building in the first picture in this section was a farmhouse after all…

'Ello, 'ello …there's a bobby actually on the beat over the railings to the left. Not that there's anything to concern him on the avenue, running across the open moor parallel with Woodhouse Lane. That could be a nanny wheeling the bassinet along the pathway where the dome of the public library, now the Feast and Firkin pub, projects above the trees.

Another area popular with mothers and young children was Woodhouse Ridge, and just such a couple can be seen here seeking shade from the sun around the turn of the century. As for those wide open spaces beyond: that curving lane running from the centre of the picture down to the right is the very same Meanwood Road which today is lined near-solid with housing and factories new and old. The houses in the distance are around the bottom of Grove Lane to the left, with Potternewton Lane climbing away to the right. Tinshill top is on the distant skyline. Picture via J. Daniels, Vesper Gate Mount, Leeds.

Samuel Smiles

There is not a lot about this building in Woodhouse to indicate that a man who became world-famous used to visit it with a few friends to give free reading lessons to adults, and provide them with library books. The Temperance Hall and Mechanics Institute was built in 1850. Samuel Smiles was born in 1812 and in 1838 he became editor of *The Leeds Times*.

The position gave him an outlet for his prolific writing on a subject which would create outrage in some sections of British society; but won him worldwide praise. Samuel's theme was that young folk must not rely on the patronage of their parents, but must cut out careers for themselves. A key part of his philosophy was that there should be an equal chance for all.

As the eldest of 11 children, he practised what he preached, although his own start in life was anything but encouraging. An accident whilst young led to a medical apprenticeship, then the taking of a medical degree at Edinburgh. But launched into the profession, he had little success: there were too many doctors.

So he set out on the travels which were to lead to him airing his progressive views in *The Leeds Times* and help to create a formidable public opinion for various Parliamentary reforms, especially of the Corn Laws, National Education and Free Libraries.

In 1842 he decided to give up what he called 'the unquiet life of newspaper work' (heaven only knows what he would have called it had he been

around today); and returned to medicine, setting-up a surgery at the end of Sydenham Terrace, Holbeck – a house since demolished.

Three years later, Samuel handed over his practice to Dr William Scott and took a job as secretary of the Leeds and Thirsk Railway. Meeting its employees at every level influenced his writings and lectures. In 1845, the young men of a Mutual Improvement Society which met in the old cholera hospital near Leeds Parish Church asked him to speak on 'The Education of the Working Classes' and he avidly pointed out how many top people in the professions, or who were successful in other fields, had started out from lowly beginnings.

Without doubt, however, the publication of his book *Self Help* was to bring him most fame; not that he sought it. Translated into 26 languages it sold 350,000 copies – a world best-seller for many years.

Despite all this, he found time on Sundays to teach young men and give addresses at the Zion School, New Wortley, which had begun in 1832 in part of a blacksmith's forge. It was later moved to Whitehall Road and had over 800 scholars. In 1937, a bronze tablet was erected at the school to commemorate him and his work.

He was, wrote H. E. Clare in the *Yorkshire Weekly Post* of 14 March 1936: 'The man who made poor boys into millionaires.' Picture: Phil Barry.

The washing, the cobbles, the homes of the workers, the church, the university; all are here in this picture of Quarry Street, Woodhouse, on 26 November 1979 – not far from that very hall where Samuel Smiles encouraged young men to consider how all these 'modern' benefits could help them progress – if they were prepared to help themselves and not simply rely on others...

Wortley

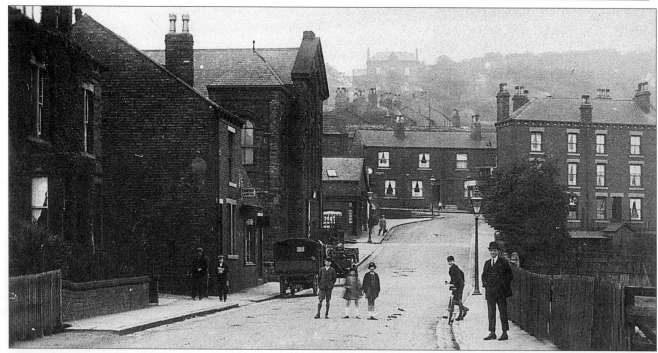

Watercourses in many great cities have long since vanished from public sight having been incorporated into their labyrinths of storm drains and sewage tunnels. However, the efforts of people living in long-established villages around Leeds to resist the local authority's efforts to 'pipe' streams such as this in their midst, meant lengths of various streams have been preserved to this day.

Farnley Beck flowed south-west after starting out close to a nearby spring at Post Hill, then performed a U-turn which brought it to a position where, today, it flows down alongside the Farnley Ring Road, through the lake at Tong Road, then becomes the Wortley Beck which goes under a bridge just about where this picture was taken in Branch Road, Wortley, in 1910. Note that neat, clean and shiny windows predominate in the local houses.

The beck served various mills in the district before becoming embroiled with the snake-like railway lines and their mass of infrastructure which dominated the area. According to the author's working map, the stream emerged again near Domestic Street, Holbeck and in the guise of the 'Hol Beck' (two words) and ran alongside Water Lane (what else?) to discharge into the River Aire near Victoria Bridge. Anyone fancy a paddle?

The Snowflakes Fire

Older people who were brought-up in a more disciplined world (it simply had to be that way for those who served in the Armed Forces, otherwise there might have been no world left worth living in); have seen a deterioration in standards which cause them to wonder what it is all about. All too often, one hears the question: "Did we really fight to allow this sort of thing?"

And older folk who suffered far more deprivation, and over a longer period of time, than members of recent generations, are baffled as to how even reasonably well-off youngsters of today can become involved in utterly senseless vandalism: even when it is members of their own generation who often suffer as a result.

These thoughts came to the author's mind when he examined the damage and graffiti surrounding this simple but striking monument in St John's churchyard at Wortley. For the smashed flagstones, broken iron railings and graffiti are around a plinth which records the names of 11 local children, aged between 9 and 13, who died as the result of an appalling incident in Wortley Church School on New Year's Day, 1891.

The headlines in the *Yorkshire Post* the following morning summed-up the tragedy: 'Shocking Affair In Leeds, Fire at an entertainment, 14 children in flames.'

For years afterwards, the memory of the dreadful scenes that night scarred the minds of all ages in dozens of local families as they recalled the 'Snowflakes Fire'.

The awful incident got its name from the part the children were to play in an evening of entertainment in aid of church funds. Mothers, aunts and sisters had assisted in the production of all-white outfits to be worn by the 15 girls in their 'Snowflakes' routine.

As friends, relations and classmates gathered in the school hall, chattering excitedly, the 'Snowflakes' squeezed into a small classroom nearby, trying not to crush their prized dresses which were made, in the main, from cotton wool. The finishing touch was to be applied by their holding small, candle-lit lanterns.

Suddenly, the chattering stopped amid the throng in the hall as piercing screams were heard. Then utter panic broke out as the 15 'Snowflakes', some ablaze from head to foot, ran screaming into the hall seeking relatives or anyone else who could help. Almost everyone was running for the exit door and there was chaos.

The vicar, Canon Bromfield, and the curate, Revd E. F. Buckton, and others tore-off coats and other garments to wrap around the children who were in flames. Both members of the clergy and several other people had their hands badly burned.

Meanwhile, the Fire Brigade had been telegraphed along with the Infirmary ambulance and the victims were soon on their way toward the latter establishment. As the news spread, people from Wortley and surrounding areas poured into the city and a big crowd gathered outside the Infirmary, seeking news of the children.

Only four survived, the others: four aged 9, three aged 11, three aged 12 and one aged 13 lost their lives and this memorial was erected by members of the congregation and friends of St John's.

The aptly-named 'Approach to Granny Lane', Wortley, around 1906. Apt, because there are probably four grandmothers in the picture; with three mothers, and seven children; or is it five plus a pair of twins; or just six, because the little girl in the bonnet in front of the shop door moved so quicky she presented two images instead of one? Points to note: the neat steps on the left at the top of Branch Road, with an extended kerb to keep water away on near-freezing mornings; and that stylish gas lamp would fetch a big price in these days of one-upmanship. No spin drier – just a clothes prop to help the sheet catch the wind; and Mr Mitchell's grocer's shop bore a set of adverts for famous British products that stood the test of time.

Eighty-nine years ago the only spice girls known worked in fields in the Far East, drugs were some sort of medicine, lipstick came from toffees when your mum could afford them and good solid shoes or boots – the latter worn by many girls – were the order of the day. But most of these girls of Standard V at Upper Wortley School in 1910 would, in their lifetimes, see the world progress and change – though not always for the better – more than it had done in the previous several hundred years.

What would come to excite them? Zip fasteners, 'Stop Me And Buy One' ice cream carts, double-deck buses, the wireless, telephones in the home, hand-rotated 'Jiffy' washing machines, toilet rolls, nylon stockings, Henry Hall and his Orchestra, Val Doonican and Clark Gable …yes, there was an interesting future for them, even if most did look a little apprehensive at the photographer's call to "Smile, please".

Almost everyone stands still at the photographer's call in Tong Road – except for the blurred figure between the tram lines. But then, he was selling papers so he had to get a move on. It was 1922 and what might appear a fearsome vehicle to young readers of today, the contraption on the left, was a tar boiler – working on one horse power. The hot tar was run off via the tap on the back, into the spouted can slung alongside. From there the workmen would pour it into any cracks they found between the cobbles. Thinks – where are all those millions cobbles which filled thousands of city and town streets in the old days? They can't all have been sold to posh folk with posh gardens down south! Note the admission prices for the 'pictures' on the right – three pence and five pence in old money; and probably a free squirt of anti-bug mixture thrown in …oh! how we kids suffered…

Those well-disciplined girls in the picture taken at Upper Wortley School would live to see a deterioration in manners, knowledge of right and wrong, and respect for other people and other people's property, by the time they had reached their 70s. It was not unusual in many inner-city suburbs, to see property that became empty from the 1960s onward quickly vandalised in a totally mindless manner; as was the old Bethel Chapel in Upper Wortley Road. Its boarded-up door offered no protection; most of its windows were bare, their fine carvings smashed; as were headstones in the burial ground, deep in the weeds of neglect and wanton damage…

Not by any means were all the children of Wortley running wild. The building pictured here was a house of dreams, hopes and care for many of them. For two years in the 1960s, the 20-room St Mary's Vicarage, New Wortley, had been home for the Revd Bruce Duncan and his wife Margaret. He was curate at St Bartholemew's Church, Armley, but had charge of St Mary's.

Nearly all the ten bedrooms were furnished and many friends of the Duncan's stayed there on a regular basis. They also provided temporary accommodation for people in need, youngsters from approved schools, students and elderly people. Scouts used one top floor bedroom for meetings and another as a store room.

Mr Duncan used another room as a carpentry workshop and yet another as an aviary where he had 25 budgerigars. A downstairs room was used by a play group. Local children were allowed to play in the grounds and, voluntarily, did many jobs around the house for the young curate and his wife. "I try to make the whole place 'open house' for the parish," he told *YEP* reporter Ron Yeomans (*who, in passing, was a wildly-enthusiastic cricket fan whose lawn was made-up of grass patches cut from various famous cricket grounds – with permission – and his garden gate was made of wickets*).

Needless to say, the Duncans were much-missed by the people who were always 'dropping in', and the various church groups who had met at their home, when they left in April 1969, on his appointment as full-time director of Children's Relief International at Cambridge. Their accommodation there was …a two-bedroom flat.

The People who made the City

Ask the average 'Loiner' of senior citizen age what concerns him or her most as we near the Millennium, and it's a fair guess the reply will include: juvenile crime, vandalism, a lack of respect by juveniles for people and/or their property, and, perhaps most importantly, the effect that all these things combined might have on their own grandchildren as they grow up.

Those concerns reveal among 'seniors' some features which their generation retains, having learned something from history and their own experiences in life; things like care, respect, concern, consideration and values.

This is not to say they consider that all today's children involved in the activities mentioned above are 'bad', but in these times when too large a proportion of children appears to their elders to be ill-disciplined, over-fed, greedy, selfish and lacking parental or other control or guidance, it is an understandable worry.

These first two pictures illustrate, quite simply, the differences between people of yesteryear who started-out with little or nothing, but at least had some pride; and some of those of today's 'I want it', couldn't-care-less generation…

Where the Loiners lived

From the last quarter of the 19th century until well into the 20th, increasing numbers of people moved from the country to the city in search of better pay and conditions, and a way of life; than they had been able to get – let alone sustain – in a mainly agricultural environment. A large proportion ended-up in Leeds slums like these. The rows of houses were often divided by high walls, as much to prevent opportunist criminals having a free run as to give some small measure of privacy. The width of the two houses on the left; almost certainly back-to-back types with only one bedroom each upstairs, was probably less than that of the average 'semi' today. No bathrooms, inside lavatories or kitchens. One outside drain to take the waste water of all who lived in the yard; all washing to be dried on lines stretched across the yard; or across the one downstairs room. The only outside light was provided by a single gas lamp beyond the wall (and note that in the next yard there is a factory whose roof vents indicate a fair proportion of escaping smoke, steam and/or fumes. But there is only one small piece of litter to be seen in the yard, other than the material around the central drain.

Now compare this picture with the last one. Over the years thousands of 'Loiners' were moved from slums similar to those in the last picture; thousands more were moved from houses with more facilities and better positions than those in that picture …and practically all of them found new homes on council estates – with adequate gardens, lots more space, trees, greenery, plentiful street lamps, kitchens, bathrooms and electrical plugs from which to run various items of domestic equipment.

Note the clean lamp and the lack of litter in Clarkson's Yard, Quarry Hill, around the turn of the century. Picture courtesy of Leeds Central Library.

Initially, whatever their financial circumstances, the greater number seemed to appreciate this better chance in life and the majority created homes just as clean, comfortable and attractive as those on many a private development.

Others, as highlighted in national newspapers, on TV and the radio around the time of writing, eventually found themselves forced-out by 'Neighbours from Hell' as the latest catch-phrase described mainly members of teenage gangs, and their little more responsible parents; who then vandalised homes like this one (and dozens more) on a Leeds estate. Where they didn't force their attentions on others, they were witless enough to turn their own homes into this sort of condition. You might well ask if some people have learned anything from the benefits of a better way of life…

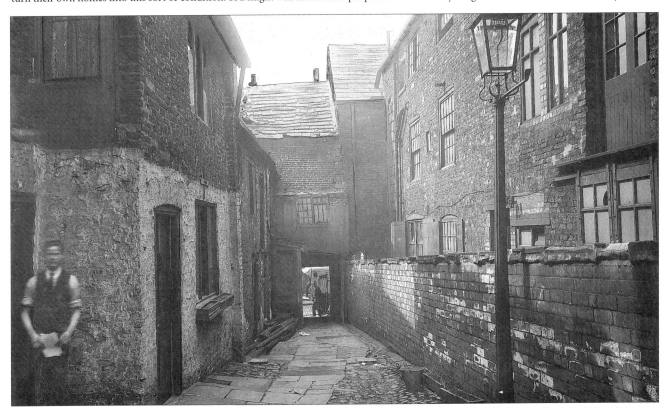

Things didn't change all that fast for some: at least two of the houses on the left of the King's Arms Yard and Atkinson Court in St Peter's Square, Quarry Hill, appeared to be still occupied in this 5 June 1924 view; but the ground on the right had been taken over for commercial use. Drainage was still via an open gutter running down through the ginnel.

Hemingway Court was typical of the many courtyards around central Leeds. Although there was plenty of evidence of deterioration in the structures and flagstones, and still but a single lamp to light two yards; and evidence of a midden on the right just past the window, people had to live somewhere. But the cat on the near left didn't look too badly fed…

Baths and Wash-houses

With many of their husbands working in heavy engineering plants and other establishments guaranteed to keep their garments anything but whiter than white, public wash-houses were a welcome feature of many a suburb. *YEP* photographer Harry Fletcher – just the sort of wag to stir things up among the lasses in such an establishment – visited the Leeds Corporation wash-house in Kirkstall Road to get this picture. Clothes were going into the washing machines at the start of a two-hour cycle which cost three shillings and sixpence.

Meanwhile, up at Armley, the gals had steamed ahead so well there was time for a laugh and a joke and invariably, a bit of leg-pulling when particularly voluminous long johns or bloomers were lifted out of the driers…

More than one comedian at Leeds Civic Theatre has used the line 'taking the plunge in Cookridge Street' to good local effect. The link was, of course, the now long-gone Cookridge Street Baths, just across the street. The building was, arguably, the most stylish of the various baths around the city.

One person who was never likely to take the plunge was this carved figure of a scantily-clad young lady swimmer set into a niche on the front wall of the baths: and this before the nine o'clock watershed…! Two tiny dogs with distinctly gargoyle-like looks about them stand guard on each side of her plinth. There to keep the pigeons off her, perhaps?

Judging by the proportions of the mill-style chimneys which rose well above the roofs of most of the swimming baths in Leeds, the Corporation must, despite swimmers moans to the contrary, have been a good customer of the Yorkshire coal field in its efforts to keep the swimming baths warm. There were many of us who suspected we were all put through the cold douse treatment, winter or summer, in those days when men were men and the woman carved on the outside wall was probably warmer than us. The chimney stack at the Union Street Baths was certainly impressive; as was the entrance building itself in April 1967; but if you examine the niche on the front wall – if you'll pardon the expression – that particular bird appears to have flown…

Good Old Schooldays

There are so many pictures of schools, schoolchildren and school activities in the *YEP* archives, a decision to use them all would take-up several volumes of this size. So we had to make a modest, random choice: but it does cover over 150 years.

The first school featured – St John's C of E Primary School, in Wetherby Road, Roundhay – was originally built by the Nicholson family, one-time owners of Roundhay Park, for children of their staff and estate workers. It closed its doors for the last time in July 1922, bringing to an end a link with education which went back more than 150 years.

A new and larger school, costing around £1 million, was built in nearby North Lane and is still in use. Between the closure of the old school and the opening of the new one, old photographs and anecdotes were being sought for possible inclusion in a book about the former. Among those which turned-up was this one of the school's Group 3, which was taken in 1904-05. That Britain was still proud of its navy was borne-out by the fact that six of the boys were wearing navy-style jackets and collars.

94

If there are any survivors of this proud little bunch of youngsters – the sports champions of Richmond Hill Church School, in 1921 – they will be a fine old age with many happy memories of that school. When this picture was first used in the *YEP*, in June 1984, one of their former teachers, Miss Dorothy Wilkinson, then in her 80s, was alive and well and living in Gargrave. A family friend, Mr Len Huff, of Moorcroft, Grassington – well-known to climbers – found the picture and sent it to the editor.

Thousands of schoolchildren found adventure, fun and a love of the countryside over the years at the Leeds Schools summer holiday camp at Windsover Farm, Ilkley. This group was approaching the breakfast tables with a set of 'doorstep' sandwiches designed to lift the spirits but weigh-down the tummy, typical of the food which kept the kids fit and well.

Mrs Ethel Bickerdike, of Park Field Row, Beeston, who supplied the picture to the editor in 1984, went to the camp with St Luke's School, Beeston Hill, in 1926 – the year this picture was taken.

She felt it typified the happiness so many local children experienced at the camps. The happiness that she gained was to be lasting: also at the farm that year was a young lad called Richard Bickerdike, from Princes Field School. She eventually married him…

Hey oop! – four years later this happy group of delicate, genteel, 'give 'im a cheer Chuck' lads from Ingram Road School, responded to the photographer's call for a cheer in great style: note that every one had a cap. Let's hope the form teacher wasn't under the scrum…

Whew! that's better …things were more orderly at Wyther Park Primary School when the photographer called in 1933. Having studied scores of such photos for various *YEP* publications over the years, the author is convinced that, whatever the year, there are several standard expressions adopted by children ''aving their pictures took' and only the style of dress changes.

Moreover, there are certain faces that change but little with time, and it would be possible to match-up several pensioners with the places where they sat or stood when this delightful picture was taken. It was supplied by Mrs Barbara Curry – née Parker – who lives in Horsforth and was fifth from the left on the front row.

When she sent the picture in, around August 1995, she could still remember some of the names and explained that the girl on the right-hand end of the front row was Margaret Lumley, who went to Australia and keeps in touch every Christmas. Funnily enough, thought the author, if there is one kid here who looks typical Aussie – it's her.

If there was one day involving children which used to grate upon the nerves of Leeds journos and Press photographers, it was Children's Day. Not because they disliked this superb event, or anything to do with children in general: it was simply that Editors, News and Picture Editors on the competing *Yorkshire Evening Post* and *Yorkshire Evening News* had a thing about being first to name, get a picture of, and squeeze as many stories as possible out of The Children's Day Queen.

Some reporters, in particular, are known to have been driven to drink – not exactly a difficult task in those rumbustious days! On 26 June 1937, – nine days after the author's birthday – the lovely Ivy Parsons, of Meanwood Road Council School, was 'captured' by a photographer outside the Town Hall – the 15th Queen in the series. Cheers Ivy, wherever you are...

A year later another photographer found this jolly group of queen's attendants (a much-prized role), preparing to board their float in Great George Street amid the chaos which ensued prior to the Children's Day Parade of 1938. Then, quick as a flash (if you'll pardon the pun), he would be into the establishment below the Tetley sign on the left for a 'nerve settler' before haring back to Albion Street with his pictures.

There were, of course, other things going on in schools in addition to preparations for Children's Day. This picture, taken at Royal Park School, Burley, in the 1950s was sent in by Geoff Craven, of Bellevue Avenue, Oakwood, in September 1992, with the news that on 3 October that year, it would be 100 years to the day when the school opened its doors for the first time. Consequently, he and other 'old boys' were organising the school's first reunion.

One of Geoff's memories of his schooldays was of going down from his parents' home in Brudenell Street – whatever the weather – to await the arrival of the Saturday evening sports papers – the *Buff* and the *Green*. Such was the competition.

It's 24 June 1968, and seven-year-old Amanda Merrikin (right) had been named Queen of Children's Day. Tracked down at Temple Newsam-Halton Infants School, Selby Road, Halton, by an intrepid *YEP* photographer, she and her attendants were allowed out of class for a few minutes for their first photograph call; but certainly not the last...

…and here is Queen Amanda again, but on the big day. She and her retinue are making their 'lap of honour' around the spectator-packed arena at Roundhay Park. Note that her single male attendant (extreme right), hasn't changed his expression since his appearance in the previous picture…But then, it's a tedious job for a lad: how will he live down this 'Queen's flunky' stuff with all his mates?

And here's one of the typical scenes from Children's Day which everyone remembers – teams of children from schools all over Leeds taking part in the wide range of activities which attracted huge crowds. Yes, it was another age and it took a lot of organising; but the rewards in terms of a job well done by teachers and others, and the pleasure it brought parents and grandparents – and not least the children themselves – made it a well-worthwhile exercise. And if you have any doubts on that score – just ask the remaining photographers who took the pictures…

At Your Service

In an age when the pros and cons of the National Health Service regularly plaster the headlines of our newspapers, flicker on our TV screens and help fill-out radio time with 'phone ins', the following quote might not seem unusual: 'Prevention is cheaper than cure …perhaps it is because it is so easy and homely and comparatively cheap that we can get very little support – people will pay more readily to cure disease than to prevent it.'

An enlightened view extracted from today's never-ending health debates? No – these words were written in 1912 to publicise the work of the Leeds Babies Welcome Association.

The benefits of preventative medicine were fully recognised by the women who founded the Association, back in 1909. Their determination led to a network of clinics, known as 'Welcomes', located throughout the city to help and support young mothers and their children.

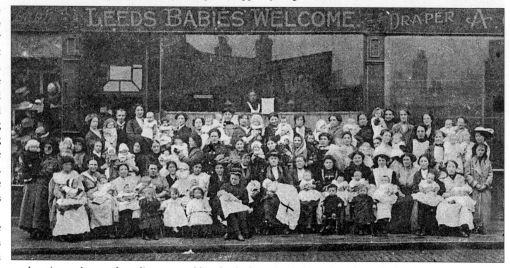

The Association disbanded in the mid-1970s, but thanks to Isobel Baylis, who was constantly hearing about 'Welcomes' whilst doing some local history research and published a history of the organisation, a picture emerged of an astonishing local organisation successfully caring for mothers and babies long before the 'National Health' came into being. So successful, in fact, that thousands of Leeds people still have fond memories of its work.

At the beginning of the century it was concern about a possible drop in population brought about by social problems – and not 'nature's way of weeding out weaklings' as had previously been thought – which led to the formation of organisations such as the Leeds Babies Welcomes.

The Leeds scheme was backed by the Lord Mayor and by Mr Henry Barran, partner in the giant Leeds clothing firm, who offered to pay the first three years' rent on premises on Ellerby Road. By 1912, there were five 'Welcomes' scattered through the poorer areas of the city, and to meet the challenge of the high birth rate after World War One, further branches were opened at Middleton, Meanwood, Harehills, Cross Gates, Burley and West Hunslet. The picture here is of the Hunslet branch.

By the early 1920s, it was claimed that one-third of all Leeds babies passed through the 'Welcomes' and 14,000 mothers were registered with the Association.

Doctors working on a voluntary basis were in attendance, but the emphasis was on education – providing advice and guidance on childcare. For instance, sanitary inspectors had found that misunderstandings and 'old wives tales' about babies' bodies were rife. 'It was often assumed that a baby's stomach was the same size as an adult's, and that it could easily digest the pobs (bread soaked in water or milk), which was often fed to them,' wrote Isobel Baylis. The feeling also prevailed that babies needed 'hardening-up', which meant they were often inadequately clothed.

Existing on a shoe-string budget, the Association set up thrift and clothing clubs for mothers. The lady who supplied the picture, some years ago (Mrs Nancy Pacey, then of Whitehawk Road, Brighton, Sussex), had the maiden name of Eden and was born on 22 February 1914, in Hutchinson Square, Dewsbury Road. She was the youngest baby on the picture and is on the knee of Lady Kitchener Clarke (centre) who opened the Hunslet Welcome.

The supermarket chain which, in 1998, announced plans for a 'home delivery' scheme was way behind the times in Mr Blaire's supposedly thoroughly modern Britain. Donkey's years ago, if the fine-looking moke here will pardon the pun, all manner of services were brought to the door in streets all over Leeds. Here is just a small selection.

The building and running of a family business could hardly be better-illustrated than in the story which Mr Fred Bentley, of Swanpool, Lincoln, sent to the editor in 1975, along with this picture which was taken in 1902-03, outside the family shop in Shakespeare Street, Burmantofts.

"The girl in the doorway is my sister who was born in 1891; brother Bill, born 1894, is holding the reins on the far side of the cart; the little fellow behind the sign is me – born in 1900. I had never had a haircut and was dressed in petticoats.

"In those days we delivered meat around the Nowells, in Harehills Lane, even though we were so young. We certainly had to work but it taught us to stand on our own two feet, and we knew all about self-discipline which is sadly-lacking today.

"Brother Bill emigrated to Canada in 1913, returning to England with the Canadian forces in 1915; whilst I served in World War One with the West Yorkshire Regiment. Bill returned to Canada after the war and died in Ontario in 1974, aged 80."

'Hygiene hysteria' and 'Mad Cow Disease' scares obviously had no effect on the Bentley family, or likely their customers, who would never have batted an eye at the way meats were presented in the shop window. Times change – and prices – the steak was selling at nine old pence a pound.

Another form of 'mobile shop' was operated by the late Mr Walter Hart, of Holbeck, pictured here with some of his customers in Cow Close Road in 1906. His greengrocery round was well-patronised, and judging by the size of his scuttle he gave good helpings. The weekly visits were looked forward to by the pinafored housewives, for he also sold rabbits and there was an unusual discount: when he came round the following week he would pay a copper or two for the skins!

One of the most popular barber shops in south Leeds was the 'Hair Cutting Saloon' of J. Duxbury, who snipped his way through over 40 years' of local locks. In this 1907 photo, Mr Duxbury is standing in the doorway with his nephew, Harry Yeoman, who at that time was an 11-year-old lather boy. The face peering through the window is probably the 'Next, please' gent, more worried about getting to the pub at opening time than 'folks 'aving their likeness tekken'.

People concerned about the proliferation of 'street furniture' and distracting signs these days, might consider what effect the mass of 'commercials' on this gable end in Domestic Street, Holbeck, might have had on a chap driving his pony and trap back from the 'local' in 1921. Various pictures – in both *Memory Lane, Leeds 1* and this new volume, underline the free-and-easy attitude to advertising in the old days. Anti-smoking campaigners of today would have been apoplectic about something like Tom Brown's Tobacco Shop appearing on their patch.

Before DIY became a hobby – or an enforcement, depending on the circumstances – there were 'certain jobs that had to be done', as the saying went. Fortunately, they required no study of pastel shades; or a shelf-laden garage looking like a cross between a joiners and a paint shop.

The major decorating tasks for many Leeds husbands, were the white-washing of cellar steps; and the inside walls of outside lavatories. The task required little study of Italian art or *House Beautiful*. So the products of the Petrosine Co Ltd, a paint and varnish company which also sold a whitewash with the lovely name of Ceilowhite were popular. And when the firm's van won first prize for the best-decorated trade van in the Holbeck Carnival of 1919, many a husband probably stifled his congratulatory cheers, realising that when the news spread, it would act as a reminder that 'there were certain jobs that had to be done…'

As for the sign on the side of the van: 'Ask for Black Cat Paints', and the cut-out cat on the cab roof: is that the cat that was seen-off by the Dulux dog?

Long before supermarkets and 'one stop shopping' were heard of, Wood's second-hand furniture store in Canaan Square, Low Road, Hunslet, had the answer: 'Sell owt – and if tha' can't get it all in't shop, stick it outside.' This was street trading par excellence: brass bedsteads, Windsor chairs, basinets, wash-hand stands, weighing scales – even a chair with what looks like a large carved crown above its large, padded back. Surely, Mr Wood was joking when he said it "came from the old queen's place on the Isle of Wight?" Mr F. Wood, of Lanshaw View, Belle Isle, who sent the picture to the *YEP* said the store, owned by his late father, also sold coal (see the sign outside the bedroom window on the right). Some of these goods, sold for a few bob in the 1920s, would probably fetch quite a bit as antiques today. And don't forget – the best stuff was probably inside.

When most of the buildings in central Leeds were a uniform black, and November fogs served one useful purpose in that they proved tram travel was far safer than travel by car in a real 'pea souper', chaps who got a living from the product which caused those problems were, nevertheless, welcome callers.

The late Mr Arthur Gomersall (standing nearest camera) of Primrose Lane, Leeds, was one of that respected breed – the coal merchant. To explain the technology for younger readers: power for the cart was provided by the 4x4 (legs) horse on the left which looked as if it had seen it all before. Mr Gomersall and his mate, in this case his brother, could sit on the seat on the front of the cart (where the youngster is sitting) when in motion.

On reaching steep hills, one of the men would 'drop off' (not literally), and apply the advanced braking system (ABS) in the form of the two skids hanging beneath the cart, which were slid beneath the leading edges of the back wheels (some Leeds trams had a similar device which skidded on the lines).

Coal was delivered in bags from the cart to houses which had a sliding grate, or cover, set in the pathway, or fixed to the bottom of the house wall. When slid open, the cover allowed coal to be tipped into the cellar below. Coal fires looked warm and cosy, but a lot of their heat was wasted when it went up the chimney and produced soot which, in turn, having risen into the sky, fell on buildings, gardens, and great-grandma's washing, causing her to be somewhat unhappy. Even so, it was better than 'being starved to death' by winters which seemed harsher in those days.

Although this Leeds City Brewery cart appears to have been decorated for a special occasion, and the horse is particularly well turned-out, it was not unusual for sales to be made from the back of a wagon. For imbibers who may be concerned about the threatened demise of Duty Free sales at airports at the time of writing, it must be galling to note that Scotch Whisky was advertised on the wagon at today's equivalent price of 80p a gallon. As the Colonel used to say in a popular World War Two radio programme: "I don't mind if I do, sir."

An Arresting List of Facts

As with most young journalists, the author spent a good deal of time reporting court cases in his early days on newspapers, and was in regular contact with the police concerning various aspects of their work. In later years, working for the old *Sunday People*, in London, he had his international crime perception sharpened considerably when he covered the capital's gangland in the company of such stalwarts as Arthur Helliwell, Duncan Webb and 'Forever Oz' Murray Sayle.

He will never forget some of his experiences which is why, in doing research for this volume, he was grateful for the loan of a fascinating book: *The Leeds Police 1836-1974*, which was produced by the Research and Planning Dept., of Leeds City Police and edited by Ewart W. Clay, a former Editor of the *Yorkshire Evening Post*. Ewart's successor, Malcolm G. Barker, reviewed the book in the *YEP* and found it contained some astonishing facts: Here are just a few:

The career of the city's first Chief Constable Mr William Heywood, was brief indeed, lasting from 1836-37. The sorry end came soon after a big fire in Water Lane, Hunslet. A few days later, a letter bearing four signatures appeared in the *Leeds Intelligencer*, which alleged that at the time the fire was at its height, Mr Heywood and two inspectors were 'drinking and tossing for grog at the Malt Shovel Inn, Meadow Lane, and

one of them was obliged to go to bed, he being unfit for duty!'

Mr Heywood, whose responsibilities included fire-fighting, had been appointed at £250 a year and had quickly gained praise for cleaning-up the streets of 'scenes of low debauchery; infamous characters annoying the inhabitants; dog fighters and gamblers.'

But when the Malt Shovel scandal broke, the following year, he was sacked after a nine-hour meeting of the Watch Committee.

In days when the use of American-style batons and disabling sprays by the police has caused much comment, it is interesting to see how the bobbies were equipped around 1840. Those on winter night duty had a tin bottle containing a pint of ready-made coffee, a pair of handcuffs, and a staff; with two pairs of white drill pantaloons and two pairs of shoes supplied a year. Forty cutlasses were held in reserve for their use.

In the Leeds Chartist disturbances of 17 August 1842, public houses were closed at 8.00pm and 30,000 staves were provided for special constables. As the Chartists started their meeting, and brought work to a halt at mills in Farnley and Wortley; 1,600 special constables were sworn-in and the 17th Lancers and the Yorkshire Regiment called out.

Then the forces of law and order set out to

intercept the mob, led by the Chief Constable, Mr Edward Read, on horseback followed by a large body of police on foot, armed with cutlasses and heavy batons. Then came 1,200 special constables with heavy batons, followed by a troop of the 17th Lancers and 18 men of the 87th Infantry with fixed bayonets. Members of the Royal Horse Artillery with a field gun came next, along with the Ripon Troop of Yeomanry. And so it went on until, in due course the Chartist troubles ended with hearings at York at which sentences of up to ten years' deportation were awarded. Australia's tourist boom was underway!

There were lighter moments: Mr Arthur Burrow Nott Bower, Chief Constable from 1881-90, had some unusual disciplinary cases to deal with: Pc347 was cautioned for smoking a clay pipe outside the chief's office. Found coming out of a tripe shop smoking instead of being on his beat cost Pc44 a fine of half-a-crown. Poor Pc241 was admonished for being found asleep in a privy. Pc82 was likewise admonished for going on parade with two black eyes; whilst Pc84 was fined five shillings for smoking and kissing a woman. Then there was Pc180 who left a fire drill without permission and was found 'performing at Edmonds Menageries, also without permission'. What he was doing is not recorded.

The Leeds force was 21 years old when its Woodhouse station was established at the corner of Woodhouse Lane and Reservoir Street. The original building was a two-storey house (pictured), used as a section station until it was demolished in 1898. In 1902 it was replaced by a large combined police/fire station and library at a cost of £6,201 10s 3d and this remained in use until 1932 when it was replaced by a police box system. This later building still stands and, although generally referred to as 'the library,' it was converted some time ago and is now best known as the 'Feast and Firkin' pub, easily recognised by its domed clock tower (see page 147 of *Memory Lane, Leeds 1*).

For many years now, judges proceeding to the courts in Leeds have enjoyed a 'motorised' police escort from their lodgings at Carr Manor in Stonegate Road. But this latter-day style is as nothing compared with the grand panoply experienced by their predecessors of nearly a century ago. This picture shows two of them about to leave the then lodgings at Little Woodhouse, at the corner of Hyde Terrace and Clarendon Road en route for the Assizes. Their carriage is about to be escorted by a detachment of the Leeds Mounted Police (left); the Judges Marshals (who were usually young barristers), seen here standing behind the two judges on the right; and the military, including buglers and coachmen.

In the Leeds Police book is a fascinating map published in 1775 which shows the then comparatively small built-up area of the city, stretching from the Leeds Bridge end of Hunslet Lane in the south, to St John's Church and Lady Lane in the north; and from the Cloth Hall (now City Square) in the west to the Parish Church in the east.

On the east side of the Sheepscar Beck was Quarry Hill with a Meeting House as a lone building on its flanks; on the city side of the beck was a stretch of open land known as Mill Garth and it was into this area that houses were crammed as industry developed. Their occupants included a large proportion of rough and tough types.

Consequently, this substantial police station costing £5,150, to be the headquarters of A Division, was built in 1878, and included a barracks and a mortuary which were, perhaps, a necessity to deal with Saturday night activity in the area. (The author recalls old Leeds coppers telling tales of how, even in the 1930s, they patrolled streets thereabouts 'in twos, sometimes sixes if needs be'.)

In 1885, the barracks were condemned by the Medical Officer of Health and the mortuary was transferred to Old Mill Lane, Hunslet in 1903. In its chequered career, the old Millgarth station opened its doors to some notorious 'heavies', plus a quota of murderers, countless thieves and enough drunks to have kept several breweries in business.

By the time the 1970s arrived, the Victorian station, with its limited accommodation, was becoming pretty cramped for the 200-odd staff and visiting 'crims', so plans were drawn-up for a new five-storey building nearby. Came the day of the big move and, at its close this constable unceremoniously nailed the 'Police Station Closed' sign on the well-worn doors.

Officially opened on Wednesday, 17 March 1976, the new building towered over the north-east end of the open market. Arriving night duty staff looked out over the area of empty stalls, quipped "Evening All", and rocked on their heels in best Jack Warner style before entering the spacious new premises. Subsequently, some of them would nick-name it 'the water chute' (because of the outer staircase); others called it 'The Lubianka' (for reasons best-known to themselves).

But in the final analysis the change was welcome, as were the facilities. And many members of the law-abiding public expressed their approval.

Other stations, too, came and went – here is the Upper Wortley 'cop shop' – up for sale in 1978. The original was used as a section station until 1898, when it was replaced by this building, combining a library, at a cost of £2,986.

A station which looked as if it could have been specially-constructed for a TV series (Oh! no – not another one, we hear the reader cry); was Chapeltown, strikingly positioned on the corner of Town Street and Harrogate Road, Chapel Allerton. The original building was used as a section station until replaced by this building in 1904. The new station incorporated a fire station and library, and in 1930 became the headquarters of 'C' Division when the Sheepscar station was closed. But times and needs changed again and in 1998 this door, too, was closed and a new divisional station opened in Stainbeck Lane.

A Great Centre of Entertainment

Having been back stage at various Leeds theatres in search of stories over the years, and being well aware that before the advent of TV the city was a great centre of theatrical entertainment, the author was nevertheless intrigued, on listening to an early-1999 radio programme featuring a number of top names in the entertainment world, just how many of them spoke with great warmth about Leeds, its theatres and its people. And the names of various 'theatricals' long gone to the great stage in the sky, were recalled as having held similar opinions.

Bearing in mind the world-wide reputation which theatres such as the Glasgow Empire had as a 'killers' that could stop young and inexperienced entertainers – especially 'comics' – in their tracks, this was praise indeed.

But it was well-deserved for the history of live theatre in Leeds is a long one; and as for the way in which 'Loiners' took to the 'pictures' – right from the very start of silent movies: few other towns or cities could compete with Leeds on a number of cinemas to total of population basis.

And so far as cinemas were concerned, it wasn't simply a case that you had to travel into the centre to have a night out at the pictures: a short tram or bus ride in almost any suburb would bring you to a cinema.

But the big downtown movie palaces were the real crowd-pullers, filling every moment with first-rate organists performing before the films started; during the intervals, and sometimes accompanying 'live' stars. And the manager who could get hold of a pair of Fred Astaire's dancing shoes; Carmen Miranda's fruit-filled hat; Charlie Chaplin's walking stick and suchlike for prize or display purposes ranked with today's successful football managers as something of a whiz-kid.

Without doubt it was the coming of TV which started the rot that led to the disappearance of most of these warm, comfortable, friendly establishments where poor families from poor homes could live their dreams in comfort, for a few coppers, over three hours or so. Subsequently, however, vast changes in the way of life of most people and not least a great increase in city centre crime has led to a falling-off in the number of people taking a night-out in town – and not necessarily just older folk.

The '24-hour-city' current 'clubbers' rage has, to some extent filled that void; with large numbers of young people travelling from as far afield as London for weekends where their kind of entertainment runs around the clock; leaving the city's Council Tax payers to pick-up the bill for the clean-up required when they have gone.

But, no doubt, something else will come along in due course to replace the current craze – there are indications already that the pace of clubbing has slowed in Manchester: which was said to have led Leeds down this road.

So, let us now get back to the days when the total of people visiting Leeds theatres and cinemas per week far exceeded the numbers of clubbers involved in weekend blow-outs …when men could imagine they were Tom Mix or Laurence Olivier; women hoped to be like Jean Harlow, if not Mae West; little girls fancied themselves as Shirley Temple and small boys …well anyone would do, so long as he was a cowboy.

The first theatre in Leeds is believed to have been this one, built by Tate Wilkinson in Hunslet Lane in 1771, and also believed to have carried the name Theatre Royal for a period. Despite his written statement that it would 'Very shortly entertain the gentlemen, ladies, etc, of Leedes with the newest and best plays, entertainments, etc, the scenes and cloathes most of them new', it was not without its problems.

The son of a clergyman, Tate Wilkinson, came under fire from the establishment in general and one vicar in particular who 'particularly inveighed against plays', wrote that great Leeds worthy Ralph Thoresby in his diary, continuing: 'which reproof was more necessary because we have had in town a company of players for six or eight weeks, which has seduced many and got an abundance of silver.'

And the early theatrical entrepeneur's troubles did not end there for worse was to come. Ordered to be transported for performing illegal marriages, he died on a convict ship. And as for his Hunslet Lane flagship enterprise: it burned down in 1876.

Another early arrival on the theatrical scene, this time in the city centre, was the Tivoli – an 1800s venture in King Charles Croft, which leaned toward music hall entertainment. On the boundary of the Red Hall and Schofield's developments (see 'The Headrow' section of this volume) it later became known as the Hippodrome but was closed down on 10 June 1933. This provided an opportunity for Snowden Schofield to extend his store premises yet again and he purchased the theatre building in 1934.

The Theatre Royal, which was to gain national fame, opened on the site of the old Amphitheatre, off King Charles' Croft, in 1878. As the years went by it was increasingly regarded as the main competitor for the Grand Theatre, but not quite so 'toffee nosed'.

Its best years were to come after 1944 when it was bought by Francis Laidler, a well-known theatrical entrepreneur, who already owned the Prince's and Alhambra theatres at Bradford; and the Keighley Hippodrome, and was governing director of Yorkshire Theatres Ltd. Productions involving his 'Sunbeams', the Tiller Girls and the Court Players would make him more famous than ever.

The success of his annual pantomimes was well-deserved and the "Oh! no he didn't" – "Oh! yes he did" routines loved by generations of children could have been invented there. The big theatrical names certainly loved it: Norman Evans regularly played the Dame in *Humpty Dumpty* and other top names of the period included Wilfred Pickles, Phyllis and Zena Dare, Peggy O'Neil and Sonny Hale.

In December 1943, excerpts from *Cinderella* at the Royal were heard all across the USA, thanks to a link-up between the BBC's Forces Programme and the Columbia Broadcasting System, as programme No.46 in the wartime series *Transatlantic Call – People to People*. Americans were introduced to the delights of flying ballets, principal boys and the Ugly Sisters, plus the Grand Theatre Symphonic Orchestra directed by Stanley C. Berkeley.

A fascinated participant was US Army sergeant Ford Kennedy, who played the part of the inquiring American, to whom everything about pantomime was explained by Leslie Mitchell, a top commentator of the time.

In November 1949, Francis Laidler made a vigorous reply to a *YEP* editorial which complained that 'Legitimate theatre in Leeds is being sacrificed for the benefit of pantomime day trippers from the whole of the north-east.'

Having fully outlined his case for a fair ticket allocation policy, Mr Laidler concluded: 'May I now be allowed to conduct my own business in my own way? That way is to present pantos that are a delight to all children – those very young and those very old.' And so say most of us.

Despite all, not even the Sunbeams could outshine the onward march of television and the Theatre Royal site (see picture on pages 113 and 115 of *Memory Lane, Leeds 1*) was sold to become part of the Schofield's Centre.

Crowds, celebrities, gaiety and regrets marked the last performance on 30 March 1957. Pictured on stage at that show, singing a chorus with the cast of the pantomime *Queen of Hearts*, are Margery Manners, Wilfred and Mabel Pickles and Barney Colehan.

It was the appearance and facilities of the Theatre Royal and the Grand Theatre and Opera House – not just the type and quality of their shows – which accentuated the rivalry between the city's two main theatres. The Royal's huge water tank, supported by a tower, gave it a mill-like appearance when seen from the street: not exactly designed to bring out a sense of anticipation and wonderment; and its rather hefty pillars upstairs required an amount of head-bobbing among children. The Grand, pictured here in April 1970, was looking somewhat dowdy, with its awful greenhouse canopy and the need for everything above it to be cleaned.

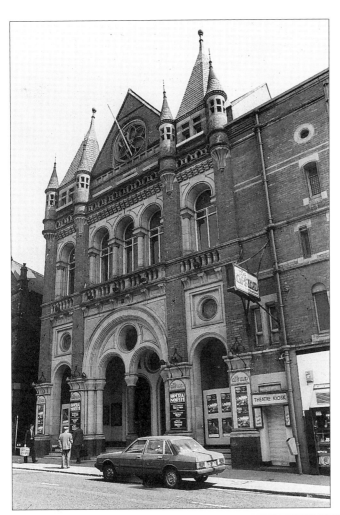

Hey presto! – it's been done, though not exactly to the wave of a wand. The Grand certainly looked more befitting of its title in this 1982 photograph, with the 'shed roof' removed and a complete face-lift in place.

However, it has always been the interior of the Grand which has helped audiences over the years to drift into another world; compared with much of what could be seen around Leeds by ordinary folks in the old days, it certainly was another world. Apart from the exotic decor – of which more in the next two pictures, it lifts the spirit and the pillars have never been quite so obtrusive as those at the Royal. This artiste's eye-view is quite remarkable in that the number of every seat – other than those unseen in the Upper Balcony's absolute 'Gods' – can be seen; although a strong magnifying glass is needed to read those at the back.

And here's a close-up of the intricate ceiling decor and the huge chandelier whose radius occupies a very large portion of the ceiling; in fact taking in almost the full width of the auditorium.

Well, would *you* buy a ticket from either of these characters? Countless thousands have done – and enjoyed laughs, magical moments, mysteries galore, daring diversions, up-and-coming singers, children's pantomimes, animal acts – you name it, it has been there. And so have world-names in showbiz for well over a century – 'way back to the good old days before the *Good Old Days* was even thought of as a top television series!

Long time friends of the author, brothers Stanley (left) and Michael Joseph, the theatre's then co-directors, were pictured when the world-famous Leeds City Varieties was put up for sale in 1987. The Joseph family had controlled the 'Verts' for nearly 50 of its 225 years' existence. A Grade Two listed building, with 686 seats, it is still in business on its supreme site bounded by The Headrow, Briggate, Swan Street and Lands Lane.

An outstanding – in all respects – memory for the author was of he and photographer colleague Irving Crawford going back stage at the 'Verts' to photograph an American women's singing group known as the 'Beefcake Trust'. Arriving at the group's dressing room, Irving's polite knock was followed by a great deal of squealing and thumping inside and there was some obvious difficulty in getting the door open.

Once inside, he and the author found themselves outnumbered and outweighed, for each of the 'girls' weighed at least 16-stones and every time one of them moved, well, everyone else had to move too: they had no choice! After much shoving and pushing "we were ejected like corks from a bottle," said Irving. The group was lined-up on the stage for a picture: the only place there was enough space!

Four pictures of the Empire Palace, better-known to most 'Loiners' as Leeds Empire (which appeared on pages 110-12 of *Memory Lane, Leeds 1*), raised a good deal of interest and generated some heartache – not least the last one showing that lovely old theatre under the hammers of the demolition men in 1962. From inquiries received subsequently, it seemed that half the population of Leeds were at the very last show, on 23 February 1961. Proof of some of those who were there on that sad occasion lies in this picture – taken that very night.

It is feasible that there were people in the audience that final night who had been present at the Grand Opening Night on Monday, 29 August 1898. If so, they could probably remember some of the acts in the programme. For those who were not there, but had grown to love a theatre which was in the great tradition of English music-hall, here is a copy of the bill, which began with 'Six Royal Welshmen' singing *God Save The Queen*, supported by the full company. After listing all the latest improvements, comes the reassurance: Elegance, safety, comfort and respectability. Yes, it was a bygone age; but there are plenty of people still alive who would gladly welcome those features back...

In the interval in this section between the demise of live theatres, and the cinemas which 'held the fort' for some years afterwards; this picture of an outdoor entertainment in Leeds featuring a world-famous character who held many a fort in his time might not come amiss.

The occasion was the visit to Leeds by the touring show which was high-lighting life in the American west. That was long before Hollywood studios began churning out westerns in numbers to rival the output achieved by today's TV companies in turning out police and hospital series.

Colonel William F. Cody, better-known as 'Buffalo Bill' after killing nearly 5,000 buffalo in eight months, for a contract to supply workers on the Kansas Pacific Railway with meat, later formed his famed Wild West Show and from 1883 this amazing attraction toured all over the USA and overseas, re-enacting famous battles and incidents.

In Leeds, before an enormous canvas backdrop, one of the incidents re-enacted by him and his touring team was the attack on the Deadwood Stage, pictured here. Crowds queued just to touch the original stage coach with its arrow scars and bullet holes. However, this was at an outdoor venue: nothing quite like it ever happened on stage at the Empire!

Lights, action, camera – onward we go from live theatre to the flickering images and piano accompaniment of the silent film era, which soon began to eat away at the audiences of theatres; as TV would eventually tempt them away from the cinemas. Here are two early posters for cinema shows at The Palace Picture House, Armley; and the Malvern Picture Palace in Beeston Road. The date of the first is unknown, the second was for films being shown around 1920. Two lines in the promotional copy are worthy of repeating: the 'Electric Theatre' film was 'First-class entertainment and free from vulgarity throughout;' the *Quo Vadis* copywriter took a somewhat different line, referring to '…gorgeous scenes, cruel massacre of the Christians, *and a love story throughout.*'

114

And here's the Malvern itself, a well-known landmark at the corner of Ashley Place and Beeston Hill. Long a family favourite with folks in the area, it was sadly missed after it closed in 1971 after being in business for around 60 years.

Those suburban cinemas were the life blood of the business in Leeds, but ask any 'Loiner' over the age of 65 which name comes to mind first when he, or she, thinks of a cinema in Leeds and it's ten to one they will answer "The Paramount". Even today there are pensioners who refer to that great block at the corner of New Briggate and the Lower Headrow by that name; after all, it was the place that put Leeds into the cinema big time – some said it made it seem that the city had got a direct line to Hollywood itself.

The Paramount opened on 22 February 1932, and 'It was a first night such as the city has never known', extolled a *YEP* writer. The chosen film for the opening, as can be seen in this picture taken the next day, was *The Smiling Lieutenant* with Maurice Chevalier, Claudette Colbert and Miriam Hopkins; backed by *The Volcano*, and the mighty Wurlitzer organ, plus a symphony orchestra.

The building went up on a site previously occupied by small shops and ale houses. The price of the 1,935 square yard site was £110,000 and the building itself cost £250,000. Despite all the talk about the 'good old days', the picture indicates that litter louts were as active then as they are today.

In due course of time, the Paramount became the Odeon and the streets were spotless when this picture was taken in September 1946, with Walt Disney's musical comedy *Make Mine Music* at the top of the bill; and Eric Lord rising from the depths on the mighty Wurlitzer. And for those who couldn't stay away from the pictures, *Beware of Pity*, with Lilli Palmer was already being advertised for the next week.

The development of the 'Odeon Twin Cinemas' concept saw the Briggate frontage getting another face lift, keeping it in line with many Hollywood stars – male and female – as this picture shows on the reopening day: 15 May 1969.

The Entertainment section of this volume began with a brief history of live theatres in Leeds, so these references to the development of this best-known cinema in Briggate link-in nicely with the history of general cinema development in the city.

As it happens, the first glimpse of moving pictures in Leeds is believed to have been at a small shop in Briggate in 1895, using Edison's Kinetoscope equipment. By 1910, early cinemas included the Easy Road Picture House, the Golden Cross Pictodrome and the Atlas at Burley. There might even be a few fans around who still remember the Theatre de Luxe, in Kirkgate; or the New Gallery; or, simply – The Picture House.

Just up the road from the Paramount, Odeon – call it what you will, the Assembly Rooms in New Briggate had long provided a quiet meeting place for genteel society. All that changed when it was transformed into the Plaza Cinema which established a reputation as a temple for torrid sex movies – as per the billboard in this shot.

The city's suburban picture palaces ranged in size from buildings which rivalled city centre cinemas, to small and cosy establishments which had enough 'back-to-backs' crowded around them to guarantee audiences big enough to keep them going. The TV 'plague', however, resulted in many of them, large and small, being converted into Bingo clubs. However, the great pile of the Queen's, in Holbeck, was still counting on Humphrey Bogart to bring 'em in when this picture was taken – with one of Yorkshire's then best-known commercial vehicles, a humble Jowett van parked outside.

One of the smaller cinemas which fell back on Bingo as a possible answer to its problems was the 'pocket size' Lyceum, in Cardigan Road.

Across town, the Capitol at Meanwood seemed to be appealing to plenty of young 'Bonnie and Clyde' types, when the film of that name with Warren Beatty and Faye Dunaway was going the rounds. But like many of the actors in the film the Capitol, too, would bite the dust in due course (see Meanwood in the *Suburbs Large and Small* section of this volume).

There were few more sad sights among the old 'suburbans' than the battered remains of the Gaiety Kinema (the 'K' was used as a preference in a number of early cinemas), at the junction of Roundhay Road and Roseville Road. Following its closure it was badly vandalised and stripped of fixtures and fittings, despite being 'bricked-up' and a steel door fitted at its once stylish entrance.

Not even Kay Kendall, Mitzi Gaynor and Gene Kelly, could save the Shaftesbury, in York Road, with their highly-successful *Les Girls* film. When this picture was taken in April 1958, the news was out that it would cease to be operated by Associated British Cinemas after their lease of the building expired in June of that year.

The Dominion (pictured), in Montreal Avenue, Chapel Allerton, opened in January 1934 with the film *Cleaning Up*, starring George Gee; and it closed on 18 March 1967, when *The Quiller Memorandum*, starring Alec Guinness and George Segal finally flickered off the screen.

Not much further up the road, The Kingsway Cinema, built in 1936, had look-ahead planners in that it had parking for 150 cars. Its first film was *Head Over Heels*, starring Jessie Matthews. But despite its modern facilities, including a very distinctive sound system; its seating for over 1,000, and well-positioned location; the Kingsway closed in August 1958, with Marlon Brando starring in its last film: *Sayonara*.

Just over a year later, following conversion, the building was reopened on 6 September 1959 as the New Vilna Synagogue, but just under 40 years after taking up that role, it was demolished for a redevelopment project believed to involve apartments.

Certainly one of the most unusual cinema buildings in Leeds, the Hillcrest Picture Lounge, Harehills, looked as if it might have been designed for a site on the front at Blackpool. But the joys and dramas it generated had already faded when this picture was taken, revealing vandalised display cabinets, windows used for stone-throwing practice (also the clock face), and long-ago-faded posters.

The fortress-like Clock Cinema, guarding the junctions of the Roundhay and Easterly Roads at Harehills was eventually overcome, like most of the other suburban cinemas, mainly by the competition of television. Pictured in September 1973, it was showing *Bridge on the River Kwai* with Alec Guinness. Its bold lines, which some described as 'the airport look' certainly caught the eye and, happily for those who have happy memories of its cinema days, its subsequent owners have retained much of its original appearance. One might almost say it fell to the enemy within, for it is now run as a popular and highly-successful electrical superstore which, needless to say, carries television sets among its products…

Posters, programmes and price lists abounded in the great days of the cinema. Every corner shop had a hanging card for some cinema or other (it usually guaranteed a couple of free tickets for the shopkeeper), and others appeared all over the place. Here are three examples of cinema publicity material.

Nowt like a day out…

No, it wasn't a fashion show, although the 'models' are worthy of closer inspection. These cheerful ladies were setting-off for an outing from the Druids Head pub in Wortley Lane, Leeds, probably around the late 1920s. There are no anorexic beanpole styles here, as thought-up by trendy London (male) designers. Should one of them have turned up at the Druids and started expounded his fashion ideas, he'd have been laughed out of the snug or given a whacking from grandma's 'gamp' (front row, right). He would certainly have been told to pull himself together "or else…" Mind you, there were one or two tricky numbers among the hats: the 'Hiawatha' (second from right, front row); the 'Jester' (middle row, beneath the Ind Coope sign); and the 'Me spacewoman, take me to your leader' (back row, extreme left). Kidding aside, there were some good-looking gals in Wortley, and smart with it. Picture from Mrs Margaret Morgan, of Bruce Gardens, Armley.

Horrendous though it was, World War Two never seemed to produce quite as much visible evidence of man's inhumanity to man as did what was originally called 'The Great War' of 1914-18. The author recalls relatives who had served in that first major conflict discussing in gruesome detail what happened in the trenches. Everyone knew someone who had been wounded; and the names of many who had paid the price with their lives. The blue uniforms of wounded soldiers were familiar to everyone living in the vicinity of Chapel Allerton Hospital; or when they were taken from there on trips to town or elsewhere.

Ladies on the staff of Matthias Robinson's store, in Briggate, formed an organisation to entertain the wounded veterans, particularly at Beckett Park. The soldiers, not all of them old by any means, were deeply grateful. One of the helpers was Miss Gladys Venables, an office junior at the time, and later as Mrs Kuhnel, of Dalton Avenue, Beeston, she forwarded this picture of just such an occasion to the editor. Note the nurse in the uniform of the day (top left). The scene certainly underscores the phrase: "Lest we forget…"

Say what you like, in the final analysis there's nowt like a day out at the seaside. There is no date on this picture which came from Mr F. Lee, of Woodlea Mount, Beeston, and depicts members of St Patrick's CYMS, Leeds on just such a jaunt. The headgear, however, might give a few clues and is interesting: near the end of the back row (left) are chaps whose hats are straight Chicago-style, prohibition period. Some splendid moustaches topped by a 'tackling look' have a distinctly Lansdown Road atmosphere about them. But wait, what's this… can that chap sitting fourth from the right on the kerb edge be… Stan Laurel? And look at the Marine Café's prices: Plaice or sole with teapot, bread and butter – 1s 6d; or with chips 1s 9d. Ham & Egg with teapot etc, 2s. As for the coach excursions (open top variety), the fare was 7s 6d; but rugs were provided.

Aha! now here's a different class of operation. No Scarborough woof and chips straight from the paper for these gents; nor a pint at The Sailor's Return. These chaps were into the Bentley, Riley, Daimler and maybe even a Rolls class – leather coats and plus-fours marking the drop-head types. Come along then, who's for the open road…? Members of the Leeds Motor Club Committee, *c*.1930s.

A proud working class

Under the heading 'For richer but not for poorer', an article in the *Yorkshire Post* of 29 March 1999 described Leeds as becoming a 'two speed city', with a booming centre bordered by communities plagued with unemployment and poverty: according to the city's annual economic statement.

Certainly, as has been described in other sections of this book, many of the great engineering works and clothing company buildings which dominated the Leeds industrial skyline for over a century have been swept away to leave wastelands, or redeveloped 'brown field' sites; leaving local communities split asunder.

Leeds is, said the report, the second largest manufacturing centre outside London and the fourth strongest retail centre in the UK; but it also forecast that the city would lose 3,000 of its 56,000 jobs over the next ten years, contributing to some 50,000 job losses likely in the Yorkshire and Humberside area as a whole.

It is a sad exercise, some would say frightening, to contemplate the run-down of highly-skilled jobs in the Leeds area over the past 50 years.

But the losses have, of course, been going on for much longer than that, even if previously at a slower place. Service industries have done

something to stem the flow of losses; but men and women now long retired from those great engineering and tailoring enterprises don't consider them as 'proper jobs', having been involved in production processes which made Leeds-made items world-famous.

But they had their tough times: periods of unemployment with nothing like today's 'benefits' to see them through; poor housing and near-poverty for long periods; and two world wars which inflicted terrible hardships on many families. But they were a proud lot: and generally loyal to their friends, neighbours, and places of work.

This bunch of likely lads were but a handful of the many thousands of skilled engineers who gave Leeds such a great reputation down the years. They were part of the workforce of the Yorkshire Patent Steam Wagon Co Ltd, of Pepper Lane, Hunslet, between 1914 and 1920: a real set of 'war winners' on the home front.

When television companies turn-out their actors – especially children – for 'Victorian drama' series, the author is not alone in noting that their 'looks' never quite ring true. This is mainly because caps, dresses, shirts, boots and suchlike, are just too fresh and tidy to ring true. But here's a picture of the real thing, taken in Club Row, Armley: date unknown but almost certainly around the turn of the century.

The two chaps sitting with their legs stretched out look as if they have just come 'off shift', and likely at a Leeds area pit. The young girls look cheerful enough but, among the older residents, hardship and disillusion come across strongly in their expressions. The rakish cap angles of the young men underline that in any generation of that age there is hope: but how about the little 'muck-tub with a face as black as t'fireback' (wearing the clogs and a distinctly off-white smock in the front row – next to the boy with the white collar). What future for him or her in an Armley where much of the housing stock was already over a hundred years old? Having said all that, the mill lasses were putting a brave and cheerful face on it...

Built in 1867 to offer the masses access to a library, a news room with daily papers and magazines, facilities where draughts and chess could be played, plus a wash room with water, soap and towels – all for one penny per week – the Working Men's Hall in Park Street had in front of it a magnificent gas lamp which gave details of the opening times (8.30am to 10.30pm). For the benefit of readers new to the city: the hall stood on the site of the current magistrates courts complex and was originally opposite the fire station. It stood the test of time and much use, being finally demolished in 1987. Just up the street from the working men's haven was another large lamp which marked the entrance to Horner's Livery Stables from which the 'nobs' could hire cabs whilst the workers headed for trams or, more likely, walked home.

Hospitals that served them...

Those who remember North Street on wet winter nights when packed trams clanked and whined down toward Sheepscar, and almost empty ones climbed back toward New Briggate to make the descent through the bright lights and warmth of Briggate, might find it hard to believe that this classy-looking house once stood at the top of North Street.

Built in the early 1700s, No.10, Town End (and the town did just about end there in those days), it was first occupied by Robert Denison and later by the Sheepshanks family. Sadly, it fell to the mixed development which turned North Street into a collection of varied businesses and, in later years, the site where No.10 had stood was used as a car park for the Leeds Public Dispensary.

The Dispensary was opened on 13 May 1904, its no-nonsense proportions giving a sense of stability and security to a medical establishment whose position had been shunted around for some 100 years.

Initially, the trustees of the House of Recovery had 'considered the proprietary of annexing a dispensary', but then decided to make it a separate institute, so the dispensary system was launched in April 1824. In the event, its location changed several times before the North Street site was acquired and a permanent establishment erected there. Throughout its working life it was best-known to most of the citizenry for its accident and casualty facilities. Renamed Centenary House, it is now the Leeds Centre for the Hard of Hearing and houses a number of other offices.

This picture, taken in June 1969, shows the substantial building at the corner of North Street and Hartley Hill. In the left foreground of the picture is the beginning of the rise from North Street up New Briggate to The Headrow.

The construction of the Inner Ring Road required a good deal of demolition work in the vicinity of the Dispensary, seen here on the right. Just behind the street lamp on the left is the turn into New York Road; with the Inner Ring Road excavation tunnelled under the road works in the middle distance where New Briggate climbs up to Merrion Street, coming in from the right just beyond the Wrens pub, with its decorative triple windows. Vicar Lane is just ahead of the car on the left of the picture and in the foreground on the extreme right is the lower end of Back Brunswick Street. Sadly long gone is the terrace of attractive shops with mock-Tudor frontages which curved up to the Wrens from just beyond the Dispensary.

This was the view looking across the bridge over the newly-constructed Inner Ring Road, with the entrance to North Street on the other side. The Accidents entrance to the Dispensary is prominent on the left and hard-by the front door is a sign revealing one of the main reasons why the new road had been built: the one directing traffic to The North (A1) and Harrogate (A61). Previously, much heavy traffic between Lancashire and East and North Yorkshire had chosen to turn Leeds city centre into what one councillor described as 'a rally route for Lancashire lorry drivers – especially The Headrow.'

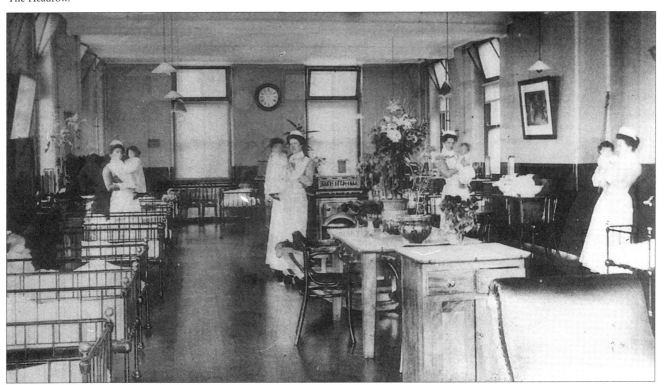

Long gone everyday scenes from some Leeds hospitals were featured in *Memory Lane, Leeds 1*. But here's another: the children's ward at St James's in the 1920s. It seems that little girls were getting special attention for this posed picture. In fact, close inspection reveals that they looked exactly like the dolls of that era, said one or two 80-year-old ladies to whom the photograph was shown by the author.

Meanwhile, the only two lads in sight are up and about: one of them on the near left by a vast chest of drawers; the other at the far end of the line of cots on the left, leaning on his hands and looking as if he's thinking: 'Girls have all the luck'. Incidentally, could that spread of greenery on the ward sister's table be 'The biggest aspidistra in the world' that Gracie Fields used to sing about...?

Another view of this famous landmark appears on the dustjacket of this publication, but as bright and breezy days are not over-frequent in the hospital world, the author felt this view of hospital staff, patients and their relatives and friends enjoying themselves at the annual gala of the Friends of Seacroft Hospital, in June 1974, was worthy of a place in this section.

It was held in the hospital grounds, hard by the clock tower built in 1903-04, and concealing a 35,000-gallon water tank. The tower reaches a height of 350ft. The event attracted a large crowd whose members obviously enjoyed the splendid summer weather and the wide variety of entertainments, stalls, and all the fun of the fair. It raised almost £1,000, making it the most successful event at Seacroft up to that time.

Religious Affairs

In Mr Blair's thoroughly modern world, it is sometimes suggested that a large proportion of the population seems to regard religion – of whatever denomination – as a thing of the past. Perhaps they have become so engrossed with some of the garbage that goes for television programming these days that they have failed to notice that for instance, at the time of writing, one of the most popular programmes of the week happens to be *Songs of Praise* on a Sunday. It is not simply a sop to delight grannies and maiden aunts, it can even attract hardened old journalists, who can think of the days of Whitsuntide parades, Sunday School Christmas parties and a nourishing cup of Bovril at the rectory when delivering the daily paper on a winter's morn. More importantly, such a programme can be a welcome reminder of the basic commonsense, decency and the ability to care still shown by a pretty big slice of the population; even in this me first, whiz-bang, anything can happen age.

But here we are concerned with looking back to the turn of the 1900-01 century, when church attendance twice a day was de rigueur for countless families on Sundays, and special occasions brought out the best in people and found them wearing their best...

Here, for instance, is a group of worshippers gathered outside North Street Baptist Church. There is nothing starchy in either the dress or attitudes of these comparatively young people, but they certainly looked like the sort of folk on whom you could depend: as many of that generation would prove in World War One.

Not far from the site of the church in the previous picture, a large crowd of Jewish residents from the North Street area gathered in 1906 for a great moment in the history of Beth Hamidrash Hogodole. Prominent among them were top-hatted business gents who had prospered in the rapidly-growing clothing trade since they, or their parents, had arrived as immigrants from Europe in the latter part of the 19th century. The occasion was the laying of the foundation stone for the Lower Brunswick Street Synagogue. In later years, as the Jewish population prospered and began to move north to better homes through Chapeltown, Roundhay, Moortown and beyond, other synagogues were built to cater for them. In due course the Lower Brunswick Street building was sold to the Salvation Army.

This group of substantial ladies enjoying a day out with another group of Baptists proves two things: 1 – roast beef and Yorkshire pudding were in; 2 – anorexia hadn't been heard of and, even if it had, its exponents would have been told "not to be so daft". As for the chap in the centre …was he someone who just happened to be passing? Or the chapel caretaker who, deep down, would have preferred to be with the lads in the back bar at the Pig and Whistle?

Perhaps the lofty heights of Brimham Rocks bore some connection with the singing of *Nearer my God to Thee*, or they just happened to be the right distance from Leeds for an afternoon's outing, for they certainly proved popular with church groups if the number of pictures of them in the *YEP* photographic library are anything to go by. Here, in the 1920s, is a party from the Sanctuary Church, Burmantofts, enjoying some Wharfedale air. Mrs E. Ambrose, then of Juniper Place, Harehills, who supplied the photo, said the group includes the church founder's son, Mr G. P. Jessom, and his wife. Also in the picture are Mrs Ambrose's brother and his wife, and two nieces.

Eating Out

The 'Continental atmosphere' apparently much-favoured by some members of the City Council in their efforts to turn Leeds into a 24-hour city (a situation which residents of some French and Belgian provincial cities might find somewhat puzzling; especially those among the working class), has attracted some support by local café owners and the likes.

But a few chairs and tables tentatively placed outside a few bars and restaurants whilst waiters rub their hands against the cold as they wait to take orders, is hardly likely to cause a stampede to buy Breton berets or Galloise cigarettes by the population in general. And brick flower containers in the precincts, overflowing with empty beer cans and lager bottles left by the previous weekend's 'clubbing' visitors, hardly help the image: but things are improving.

On the other hand, Leeds has come a long way in the restaurant stakes and a trawl through the files marked 'Restaurants' in the *YEP* picture library reveals that an almost bewildering variety of establishments is now in business in the city centre and suburbs: enough to please connoisseurs from many countries.

The days when the most popular restaurants and cafés were in the city centre, probably less than 40, mostly serving good, straight-forward Yorkshire fare, are long gone. And so have the days when only the occasional fish and chip shop saved visiting strangers in the suburbs from actual night starvation…

In those days it was essential that the best-known 'posh' places had to have foreign-sounding names. The Jacomelli establishment, pictured here, at the corner of Upper Mill Hill and Boar Lane, was popular with the management set at lunchtimes, and would not have looked-out of place on New York's Upper East Side.

For the cocktail time set, Powolny's, on Bond Street (conveniently just across the street from the then Yorkshire Conservative Newspaper Company's headquarters), had an up-market restaurant; although in this 13 January 1961 photo, its outward face was past its best and its colourful appearance only came into view when the electric sign was switched on.

Known simply as Polly's Bar, journalists from across the street – who drank beer, not cocktails (their pockets rarely full enough to meet its fancy drinks and restaurant prices) – were among the more regular attenders at its 'ordinary' bar. And even more so in later years when it became Yates' Wine Lodge – 'A Blackpool company', sniffed some of the Powolny's set.

But the delights, and after effects, of South African Cape White Wine could be experienced at prices which would barely buy a box of matches these days.

At first glance, the stranger strolling along this Headingley street might well be forgiven for thinking he is looking up the garden of some eccentric householder who has sought safety for his garden gnomes by putting them over the front door. But amidst the ivy above them is the sign that has brought international fame for this modest-looking establishing: Bretts Fish Restaurant.

Back in 1976, faced with a possible barrage of six-hit complaints over the radio from the world's top cricket writers, and broadcasters, Leeds City Council decided to release several properties in Headingley from its housing clearance programme. Among them was Bretts and, next door, Hanson's painting and decorating business. Both had then been in North Lane for 57 years.

The decision brought a great sigh of relief from the Press Box at Headingley cricket ground, when it was confirmed that the rumbling tums of household name cricket experts from Leeds to Sydney could continue to be placated with plates of fish and chips at nearby Bretts, following Test and other matches.

On one occasion, a top broadcaster, who had done his homework, happened to mention over the air that the best fish and chips in the world came from a shop within 11 miles of Bradford Town Hall. All hell broke loose, especially among the fish 'n' chip fraternity in Leeds. But peace was restored when the broadcaster revealed that, as the crow flies, Bretts came just inside the 11-mile radius. Honour was restored to North Lane and Leeds. Threats to batter and fry the broadcaster until well done were dropped.

A tranquil scene not 11 miles from either the Leeds or Bradford town halls. Low Hall, Horsforth, was one of the most popular restaurants in the area 20 years ago, set in the slice of countryside that remains between the two cities. Details of its history appear in the Horsforth section of the chapter on suburbs in this edition…

The Leeds Pals

Countless people must have scorned whoever it was who described World War One as 'The war to end all wars'. But such was the size of most aspects of that conflict – practically everything was on a scale that had never been seen before – that perhaps the originator of that phrase could be forgiven for thinking that nothing like its horror, loss of life, cost and the wiping-out of a large slice of a whole generation of young men could ever be seen again.

Look at the face of the young man pictured here – little more than a boy with a sense of innocence so strong as to make it hard to believe he was going to war. Yet he was just one of many such young soldiers in the 15th Battalion, the West Yorkshire Regiment – the 'Leeds Pals'. These were World War One heroes; their patriotism and optimism still fondly remembered, but by an ever-decreasing number of colleagues, friends and relations.

The bravery of this gallant band of Tykes, most of whom sacrificed their lives on a foreign field, is the stuff of legend.

From the soot, crowded streets, busy factories and coal mines of the Leeds area, the 'Pals' were moved out to Colsterdale – probably the first glimpse many of them had of real countryside and the wide open spaces of the moors. And for too many, it would be almost their last. Here are some of them lining-up for inspection on arrival in camp, their sole items of 'uniform' being bulging kit bags and cloth caps. Some of the 'men' in this picture were little more than boys; nervous, apprehensive, but determined to do their duty and have a go at the 'Hun'.

Once they reached their tents, the lads were able to relax somewhat and appreciate the beauty of the countryside surrounding them. Pipes were lit, and overcoats taken off; but one or two of the smiles looked a little forced.

It would not be long before they were transformed into soldiers and sent off to France. For many of them it would be a short war, for on 1 July 1916, The Pals were virtually wiped-out in the Battle of the Somme.

Other cities, towns and rural areas where local regiments were raised suffered similar casualties. In due course war memorials listing the names of the dead and missing were erected in their home areas in tribute to their gallantry; but whilst not decrying their courage, some doubted the wisdom of a system which, although it might have helped morale, resulted in the virtual loss of a generation of so many young men from the same areas; leaving a host of grieving parents, young widows and fatherless children like a human blight on the local landscape.

What they fought for… what they left behind… this cairn, set in the glory of Colsterdale, is all there is left at that first campsite to remind present and future generations what The Leeds Pals did for them. On a glorious day a few survivors of that lost youth, by then pensioners with a host of sad – and some happy – memories, bow their heads as prayers are said before a two minutes' silence for their fallen Pals…

In October 1993, veteran ex-servicemen were in Leeds for a nine-day international commemoration, launched by the city council and Leeds University to mark the outbreak of World War One. Leeds-born Bill Towers, then aged 95, on the left of this photograph, had served with the Royal Field Artillery from 1914 to 1917 when he was 'blown-up' and lost a leg at Passchendaele. Despite his age, he delighted in 'inspecting' living historians of The Great War Society, who were in City Square in uniforms of the 1914-18 period. Bill, who went with the British First Army 'to wherever there was trouble', was born in Harehills and volunteered for service in November 1914. At the time this picture was taken he was living in an old people's home at Blackpool.

Although the Leeds Pals were the best-remembered local unit, they were not the only one. Pictured at Cape Town, where they had arrived in 1900 for duty in the Boer War, are men of the 4th West Yorkshire Militia. Unfortunately, the caption which accompanied this picture has been partly destroyed but it is known that among this group are three brothers and their father from the same family. In all, the father had ten children and, unhappily for them, he died in 1907 from the effects of a head wound sustained in South Africa.

But prior to that, on his return to England, he and his wife ran a small shop in Stainer Lane, Leeds, where they supplied food 'on tick' to foundry hands at a nearby works every lunchtime. But the men always paid-up when calling at the shop before going home on pay day.

One of those ten children as the proud keeper of a precious souvenir sent from his father to his mother whilst he was in South Africa. It was a silver wattle leaf with a message inscribed upon it and came from a tree on the side of Table Mountain.

A fine mix of pubs

Under the heading 'A Pride of Pubs', the section referring to such establishments in *Memory Lane, Leeds 1*, attracted almost as much correspondence and 'phone calls as any other section in that first volume. The author, who has been known to enjoy a touch of Tetley's – and other Yorkshire brews

– wasn't surprised; for as any journalist old enough to remember the days before electronic media literally trapped many of their successors in today's news rooms; if you wanted to find a story in the old days, the pub was the place to go.

Bar room (friendly) arguments and everyday banter range across the vast number of goings on in a city the size of Leeds; and the many attractive pubs in the countryside beyond are also valuable sources of information which, filtered through attentive ears, can provide lots of good stories. Likewise, before we all became part and parcel of metal boxes with four wheels, the upper decks of busy buses were gold mines of information to the listening 'journo.'

So let's take an imaginary pub crawl, in the nicest possible way, through the streets of the city and beyond and see what pubs can tell us – especially about themselves.

The ginnels of Briggate provide a fertile hunting ground for the pub seeker, even when only a handful of yards remain out of the 52 (yards, not pubs) which were once located behind Briggate. This charming little pen and ink drawing, origin unknown, is of the Pack Horse Inn almost in its original form. More about that one later…

The Old White Horse Inn, which stood on Boar Lane, was a pull-up for stage coaches long before the trams rock-and-rolled their way twixt Briggate and City Square.

It is more than likely that some of the stage coaches which conveyed travellers to and from the Old White Horse passed one of the most notable landmarks in East Leeds: namely the Old Red Lion which is situated on the left-hand side of York Road as it leaves the city. It was old even when this picture was taken in 1902 and, as the sign on the left shows, Sarah Ann Dobson was in command of proceedings. It had a somewhat run-down appearance in those days but the stonework has been renovated and much of the structure refurbished so that now it presents a much more welcoming appearance. The only thing against it in these marketing conscious days is that having crawled around the Ring Road, or through heavy traffic on the way up from the city centre, non-local drivers are likely to put their feet down hard on the straight just before reaching the Old Red Lion and pass it with their modern horse-power going full out...

The caption with this picture quotes a view of the Old Mexbro' Arms, Chapeltown Road, as it was between 1706 and 1924, and lists its tenants in that period as having the names Hill, Swales, Riddle, Atterton, Robinson and Baker. Certainly, the pub is still recognisable although the tram lines and cobbles are long gone. Note once again a flagpole there for patriotic occasions...

Back in Lower Briggate, the Old George Hotel, on the east side of the street, appears to be taking on a distinct leaning to port; unless it was that the photographer had been at the Tetley's (advertised in the window) before he set-up his tripod. As a commercial hotel, the George must have had rooms – and possibly a restaurant, for the curious sign between the upper storey windows seems to be made up of loaves of bread, a sheaf of corn and an oversize bunch of grapes. Simpson's wine and spirit merchants were also on the premises (via the ginnel on the right) and for more genteel travellers who preferred to keep some distance between themselves and the Tetley's, there were tea rooms on the left. The Old George closed in 1919.

Such is the curious island site of this old pub that even ancient 'Loiners' among the tap room fraternity would-be hard-pressed to say exactly where it used to stand. The fact that the whole area around it has been developed and redeveloped several times since the 1930s doesn't help. So, picture the south side of Eastgate where it reaches the bottom of the slope from Vicar Lane and roads now hurry traffic in all directions. The front of the Old Marquis of Granby, seen here, was on St Peter's Street, on the east side of which Quarry Hill Flats were later built.

The original pub had been licensed ever since the Licensing Act of 1872 and for many years it sold home-brewed beer made on the premises (note the barrel hanging from the crane on the right-hand side of the building), the then landlord, Mr John Spencer, making his last brew in 1931. Prior to that he turned-out 400 gallons a week.

The photograph came to the *YEP* from Mrs Maud Spencer, then living at Annums Close, Thornton Dale, near Pickering, whose late husband, Norman, was the son of John Spencer. The latter finally called "Time" for the last time on 9 February 1933, the pub closing for good in order to be demolished to make way for road improvements. Its brewing and bottling plant was sold as scrap iron. A *YEP* report that February said that the day after the closure, a new 'Marquis' would be opened in a palatial new building on the opposite side of the road.

Looking, to some extent, as if it had lost hope, the Hope Inn pictured in the 1880s amongst this sea of cobble stones was at the junction of New York Road and Vicar Lane. The large and graceful building set back from the road on the right you should, dear reader, have seen already in the section titled 'Hospitals that served them', for this was no less than No.10, Town End – better-known as the Sheepshanks House – on the site which was later used as a car park for the Leeds Public Dispensary.

Whether the top-hatted gent with the well-dressed ladies standing by the massive gate post was Mr Sheepshanks himself is not known.

Taken around 1900, this picture of the Leopard Hotel, in Wheatsheaf Yard between Briggate and Land's Lane, indicates that the building was in need of some care and maintenance. Though not an exactly up-market tavern, the pub attracted some respectable folk who liked to sport hefty watch fobs

and chains and knew how to clean their boots and shoes (an attribute not too evident in 1999). The two school lads on the right are well-scrubbed and attired and the lass sitting on the steps – probably a barmaid, would not look out of place in some of the city centre's present day bars. The pub, incidentally, was demolished years ago.

Going back to our starting point in this section, the Pack Horse had not changed a great deal from its depiction in that drawing at the start, to when this photograph was taken many years later. Some of the window frames had been changed; the glass wall of a 'studio' had risen to the left and a splendid gas lantern bearing the name Pack Horse Inn had appeared above the bay window. Many a tall tale was told by journalists and photographers from the Leeds papers when they packed-up on Friday evenings and trotted off to the Pack Horse, which usually marked the start of a pub tour on foot followed by a tram ride to home or 'digs'.

In this undated photo, the well-proportioned, no-nonsense frontage of the Lion & Lamb looked out across the York Road at Seacroft. Its two signs announced that it sold home-brewed beer and that the landlord was Ronald Stuart McNeill. Originally, this was the site of the Old Lamb Guest House which was sold in 1931 to a Birmingham brewery; closed in the early 1950s, reopened as the Seacroft in 1958, then changed back to the Lion and Lamb in 1983 'by public demand.'

Not a thousand miles from the Old Marquis of Granby, mentioned earlier, was the old Yorkshire Hussar, stuck amid a huddle of terrace houses. This picture was one of a series taken specially for the Leeds City Improvement Trust, to show the bad housing and insanitary conditions which prevailed at the time (there were undoubtedly far worse examples than this). The photographer was Henry Dixon, famous for his photographs of Victorian London, and this special collection of old Leeds pictures was eventually put up for sale at Sotheby's.

Now, if ever there was a pub that one might have expected some wealthy American to buy up and transfer tile-by-numbered-tile to the side of a desert road in Nevada or New Mexico, it is this one, for it is a real one-off. More important: it is still in business – as is. Hunslet's magnificent Garden Gate had its very own polished tile frontage designed and manufactured to make it outstanding on what was a busy road until Hunslet, as described elsewhere in this volume, was redeveloped until it was almost unrecognisable and the 'Gate' found itself in one of these new-fangled precincts with not a tram in sight.

But such is the fame of this establishment, and the quality of its ale, that it is still as busy as ever. The magnificent bar, also pictured here, had its own unique design, and apart from the intrusion of the dreaded TV set, has hardly changed since it was built.

The pub sign outside sports a miniature gate but a genuine, 100 per cent Leeds 'Loiner' needs no sign to tell him this is a Tetley house. Inside there are a number of well-appointed rooms; comfortable, warm in winter but, as it seems able to provoke a slight twitching of the noses of true Tetley drinkers over ten miles away, you know whose house it is the minute you open the door, for as in most of the older pubs of the Hunslet Lane brewery, the majority of its customers – especially the blokes – prefer to stand in the passage!

We started this pub tour via the ginnels, alleyways and courtyards of the city centre; we end it in similar fashion in the long since gone Kenyon's Court: blocked-off by Myers's Temperance Hotel. Strangers to Leeds in search of a pint might have found that as shocking an experience as did the Australian song writer in the scorching outback who was moved to write the famous Aussie song: *The pub with no beer*… Cheers everyone.

Something to celebrate

It's the 26th of May 1906, and Hunslet Carnival is ready for the off, with the local 'royals' taking up their positions on what looks like the stand of the local rugby ground. The 'Dowager May Queen' (Miss Ellis); the new May Queen (Miss Nixon) and their Maids-of-Honour are pictured. Not mentioned are the four lads – two in tricorn hats, two in sailor hats of the period – who probably took some stick from their mates in later years when their mothers dug-out this picture of the 'maids'!

Bearing in mind that the sign over his shop described Mr H. Grimshaw as a decorator, it seems he wasn't joining his fellow shopkeepers in their decorative efforts at Farsley on Coronation Day (King George V) in 1911. E. Skelton's fent shop next door had gone to town with the bunting (possibly made on the premises, as 'fent' was the name given to odd and short pieces and remnants of cloth). Beyond them the proprietor of the sweets, tobacco and high-class stationery shop featured Lambert and Butler's Waverley Mixture and Log Cabin Tobacco among his smoker's requisites. A cheeky wind was causing a flutter among the bunting, and those flying saucer hats worn by the girls were taking some controlling.

Thinking, perhaps, of loved ones who would never return to Rydal Street, Beeston, following World War One, a few of those pictured at the street's 'Peace Tea' in 1918, did not seem happy. But some folks had gone to great efforts to make sure that, however it started, the tea would develop into a happy occasion. Folded paper Union Flags had been transformed into hats, fresh flowers had been put into a vase to form the centre-piece of the neatly laid-out table that would soon groan under the weight of food put out to celebrate the ending of hostilities. This photographic record of social history in Beeston was found in the early 1990s by Tony Geary, an antiques dealer with premises in Richardshaw Lane, Pudsey. He found it in some furniture he had bought and promptly handed it over to Gerry Tomlinson, owner of Memorabilia.

There's more patriotism evident in this picture of the good ship *All British*, about to be launched into the Lord Mayor's Civic Parade of 1920; albeit on a lorry believed to have been loaned by Heaps Arnold and Heaps.

This gallant band of Hunslet Pikemen, or was it the Holbeck 21st Men-at-Arms, or the Stourton Light Infantry? had more likely travelled by special trams rather than marched over Leeds Bridge to Roundhay Park when, as pupils of Hunslet schools, they joined the city's 300th Anniversary Celebrations Pageant at Roundhay in 1926. Pictures like this make one realise what a wonderful asset the park has been to Leeds over the years. Generations of 'Loiners' have, as children, taken part in various events in that superb arena. We should treasure it – and treat it with the respect it deserves.

Arguably an even greater treasure for the city, and one which probably deserves more attention and thought given to its use than has been evident in recent years, is Kirkstall Abbey. Why, for instance, has no effort been made recently to have one of the popular BBC *Songs of Praise* programmes broadcast from there? As a setting, it would excel for that purpose: just as it did when this picture was taken during the course of the Leeds Tercentenary Celebrations.

The Grand Opening for the Tercentenary Celebrations of 1926 took place at the War Memorial – referred to by many as the Cenotaph – in City Square, where the huge crowd soon had the tram drivers whirring their sock-covered brake handles around. As can be seen, particularly on the tram on the left, the vehicles were crammed with passengers – especially on the upstairs balconies which afforded a splendid view of the proceedings. In the background, behind the rather grand memorial gateway, was the Wellington Station.

Time marches on, but patriotic 'Loiners' had lost none of their enthusiasm for the royal family (who, to this day, are reputed to place Yorkshire high on the list of places they delight in visiting), when residents of Bramley organised this street party in May 1937, to mark the Coronation of King George VI. One thing is for sure, if the marketing department at Oxo catch sight of the glasses worn by several youngsters in this picture, they will likely be tempted to try this kind of publicity again! It could be something of which HM The Queen Mother would cheerily approve…

The residents of Kirkdale Drive, off Wortley Road, needed no commercial help from outside when they entered a Best Decorated Street Competition to mark the Coronation of the present Queen in 1953. Not only did they display the astonishing neighbourly attitude and pride that were a feature of the majority of Leeds districts, they ran a group do-it-yourself effort involving adults and children alike to make their own decorations (pictured), which won them the contest! Individual houses, porches, fences, even the street lamps and telephone poles were decorated in a splendid joint effort which underlined the old phrase that "when Yorkshire gets down to it, it does t'job reight."

More recently, 'in-comers' to the city have been imbued with that sense of Yorkshire pride and the desire to put on a good show: in this case one with a Afro-Carribean accent. A no-nonsense Leeds City Transport double-deck bus; complete with driver, conductor, open platform at the back, route indicators back and front and the name Leyland on the radiator (which gave it as much standing in the commercial transport world as did Rolls-Royce in the posh car market), is marooned in a sea of celebrating citizens in Chapeltown Road, en route from Potternewton Park towards the city centre. Hundreds joined in the dancing parade as Mardis Gras burst out in West Indies style: it was a wonder someone didn't have the bus driver out of his cab to join in – for in almost every one of these annual events, at least one copper has been nabbed to swing and sway; proving that our policemen really are wonderful. Yes, it's all a part of having something to celebrate.

The Ever-changing City

More yards, courts and ginnels

The maze of yards, courts, ginnels and passageways which spread like tentacles off Briggate and other main streets made the city centre 'something of a mystery packet' to strangers, but they were a real benefit to citizens who wanted to move quickly from one part of the centre to another, and partly under cover in inclement weather, before the covered arcades became established features.

This was the Briggate entrance to the Rose and Crown Yard in 1888, with a sign above the ginnel on the right proclaiming the presence (up the yard) of J. Binks's Rose & Crown Hotel, a picture of which appeared on page 61 of *Memory Lane, Leeds 1*. In due course the yard was replaced by the Queen's Arcade.

Wormald's Yard, off lower Briggate, survived to a fairly late date as can be seen by the bonnet of the Morris Minor on the far side of the archway. The building with the arch was quite ancient, those nearer the camera less so; as indicated by their adornment with fall pipes, telephone extension wires, gas pipes and a gas lamp.

Despite the popularity of the word 'modern' with some politicians (who use it as if modernity had only just been discovered); and an urge for constant change and a 'go faster' mentality in the world of business – particularly electronics, science, computers and communications – it is nice to record that despite the '24-hour city' syndrome much admired by some city councillors, Leeds manages to retain something of its proud past in its central area.

Yes, there are changes – and increasing numbers of new buildings have broken away from the boring, red brick 'Salford Quays look' of a few years ago, to present individualistic faces to the populace.

But it is outside the central area – particularly south of the river – that the changes which began with the clearances required by the coming of the motorways are going on apace, with an ever-changing skyline showing the effect that these exciting developments are having – and will continue to have – in order to meet the demands of business and commerce, transport, and not least the people, as we move into the 21st century.

The 'Loiners' who thought they knew their city are going to have to think again, and go out and about on journeys of reacquaintance, for memories are being overtaken by events, and some surprising jolts can be encountered.

For the moment though, let us take another stroll back in time, via photographs of areas and structures once familiar, but now lost in whatever it is that drives this ever-changing city.

The building on the left-hand side of Dodsworth Court looked in this view a little like a prison block; not that shoppers and commuters would take much notice as they hurried from offices and shops around Albion Street and Trinity Street to catch their trams home from Briggate. Trinity Street, obliterated in the changes which took place in this area of the city, once housed the offices and printing works of the old *Yorkshire Evening News*. The sight of the big presses running full-out in the basement, especially when they were printing the Saturday *Green 'Un* sports paper, was a big attraction for small boys in the old days.

Well-worn steps below the doorway on the left are just out of the sunshine which streams down Russell Street, running between Park Row and East Parade, in this 1945 picture. This set of ginnels was a handy short cut to City Station for office staffs working in that section of the city. The girl in the picture is just crossing the lower, west end extension of Bond Street, with Infirmary Street beyond the parked cars in the distance.

The Victoria Arcade, twixt The Headrow and Land's Lane, was anything but an alley or ginnel, but it served a similar purpose in that it was a first class shelter between those points on rainy days. The distinguished name of Schofield (a name which eventually dominated this block to the extent that many referred to 'Schofield's Arcade' rather than giving it its proper name), was highly-respected and the window displays revealed some class. The ladies' underwear department (pictured) was oft-referred to as the 'Pull up thi' top gallants, Nellie, Department', by an old Leeds journalist as he surveyed displays of massive corsetry on his way for a lunchtime drink at the King Charles pub after a morning covering court cases at the Town Hall.

147

By the 1960s, the west end of Leeds city centre had been cleared of many snickets, ginnels, alleys and the old properties around them. This resulted in a vast open space at the junction of Westgate and Park Lane, allowing for a king-sized roundabout. Shortly afterwards the builders arrived to start work on the city's International Pool. Here are some of them securing the first of two 180ft long girders, each weighing 40 tons, which were mounted diagonally across the pool at a height of 75ft.

Some would argue that the roundabout near the International Pool, which dominated what was one of the largest open spaces in the west end, was preferable to what succeeded it: i.e. the cuttings, bridges, slip roads, tunnels and infrastructure which brought clutter back to an area which, for a period, had been a joy to behold and drive around. The proof lies with this picture: just compare it with the morning scene around this area on any current weekday…

Slum Clearance & General Demolition

Taking an overall view, 150 years ago Leeds was probably no worse off than any other regional British city in terms of slum housing. Taking a narrower view, because Leeds possibly had fewer areas of middle to upper-class terraces and parades than there were in some cities, it might have given the impression to visitors that slums dominated the inner city districts of Leeds.

Agricultural workers and their families who had flooded into the city when the Industrial Revolution set-off a boom, particularly in the clothing and engineering trades, were inclined to seek homes within easy reach of their

workplaces and, wages being what they were, they would put-up with jam-packed conditions in tiny homes that were little better, if at all, than those they had left in rural areas. And at least the latter enjoyed some fresh air, whereas the stink in some central areas of the city was with them 24 hours a day.

Products advertised in today's newspapers, particularly the Friday 'electrical bargains' pages, contain what are now everyday use items, but were once as remote from the slum dwellers of Leeds as was the moon itself. Housewives, particular those with large

families – which in many streets, yards and courts was the norm – toiled long hours every day with primitive washing, cooking, toilet and other facilities which are now almost unknown – even in some Third World countries. But if there was one good thing which these conditions bred outside of vermin and disease, it was a tightly-knit sense of community where people were always ready to help out when others were in difficulties; even if they were fully-stretched themselves. A far cry indeed from the 'me first' atmosphere that prevails in all too many suburbs today.

Those fortunate enough to live on the sunny side of Tab Street, which led up to St Mary's Church, could engage in the practice of 'taking a breather' on their front steps, between bouts of household chores. By night – try to imagine it in our, 'sophisticated age' of unsafe streets – a single gas lamp (near the top on the left) provided the only light to lead folks home.

The only 'transport' available was a flat cart, parked outside the owner's door on the right, and a built out of a box kids' wheelbarrow in the left foreground. The poor quality of the bricks shows-up clearly on the houses on the left where zigzag lines of pointing reveal attempts at waterproofing. Nearly every bedroom window in the street is half open to 'get some air in…'

Pictured from North Street, this was Hope Street, which eventually gave way to New York Road. Those living in the gloomy dwellings on the right were no doubt living eagerly in the hope that, as in Copenhagen Street going off to the left, and the properties beyond with smashed windows and the like; they would soon be moved out and their three storey dwellings left to the demolition men. Note again – just one street lamp for this whole area. But there must have been a bit of brass about; the posters on the left include one by the Great Northern Railway advertising trips to London; Cook's Midland Railway Excursions board was bare – they probably knew the locals were on the way out. For those strapped for cash, Oxford Place Chapel was advertising admission free Happy Saturday Nights with 'Music Pictures and Recitals'.

As the years went by, the pace of slum clearance quickened, aided by increasing numbers of mechanical devices and these quickly turned packed, bug and rat-ridden, outside lavatory, open-drain yards and houses packed higgledy-piggledy in every direction, into wide-open spaces where the wind blew unhindered for the first time in a couple of hundred years. This was a section of Burmantofts, opened-up to the skies again, in 1967.

In view of what has been going on in the Balkans over the past several weeks at the time of writing, younger readers will not be surprised to learn that, for various reasons, wars cause housing shortages and once the fighting is finished, people like to get back to normal as quickly as possible. And the number one part of being normal is to have a house.

Unfortunately, wars also create shortages of skilled employees and materials so, after World War Two ended, someone came up with the brilliant idea of prefabricated houses, built from sections which could be manufactured in factories, then taken to the housing site and quickly erected. Between 1946 and 1949, a total of 1,210 temporary bungalows – or 'prefabs' as they were best-known – was built in Leeds to help ease the post-war housing shortage.

The word 'temporary' turned out to be something of a misnomer because continuing shortages, and the popularity of the prefabs meant that many were still in use well into the 1950s and beyond: some tenants even bought them and stayed on even longer.

The butt of many jokes and complaints, the prefabs were, none the less, popular with many tenants. After all, if you had been born and spent your early years in a tiny back-to-back, with no kitchen, bath, hot water system or inside lavatory; a dwelling which had all these facilities – and more – under one roof, just had to be an improvement.

The prefabs pictured here were in Crossfield Street, on the St Mark's Estate, Woodhouse, in October 1955.

It was not, of course, simply the demolition of the slums and old factories which changed the face of Leeds throughout this century. Some well-known and quite distinguished buildings also fell to the demolition crews. Here a famous landmark, Priestley Hall, in Park Row on the fringe of City Square, bit the dust as they and the developers combined to allow new structures to appear. Commuters hurrying to and from Leeds Station – without the aid of alleyways and ginnels to speed them on their way – now pass the new buildings on this site with rarely a second glance.

Things were not going swimmingly at Cookridge Street Baths when this photograph was taken. All that remained of the baths and various other offices and suchlike on the site, is spread out in the foreground. Demolition had come downtown and the site became a popular and handy car park. But just look at the condition of the Leeds Institute – as was – in the background. It hardly looked the setting for the bright lights of the Civic Theatre with that inky coat of good old Leeds soot over its face. But now check out its shining morning, and evening face on the next photo…

"Aye, there's nowt about any Leeds building that a good scrub down won't improve", they used to say and here's the splendid new face of the Institute-cum-Civic Theatre, complete with some rather theatrical lamps and a bright display of flowers. A pity, though, that they didn't spend a bit more and get those cracks pointed-up on the steps…

Bangkok? Mexico City? Heckmondwike? Wrong on all counts. This was known as the 'Allotment Jungle' and made some passengers arriving at the nearby City Station pleased that they had purchased return tickets so that if the natives got restless, they could flee back to Bristol, or wherever. Although the author does not rejoice at everything the developers have done to brighten-up the face of Leeds, developments in the area adjacent to the station have displayed some careful thinking, good design and a generally pleasing appearance: far better than the 'Salford Quays look' which, up to the early 1990s, was giving the city a disappointing look-alike appearance of the brick-built horrors which stand not a thousand miles from central Manchester. Most of it, of course, had to be red brick …being Lancashire.

Whether demolition King Fred Dibnah was behind this splendid entertainment for small boys is not known, but there was obviously something else going on that day in January 1975; or the weather was bad when this 60-year-old eight-sided chimney was felled on what had been part of Whittaker's Brickworks site at Elland Road. Possibly Leeds United were at home? – for there was only a handful of spectators to see the 135ft chimney come down. The clearance of the site was part of the contract for the South-Western Motorway which, at that time, was scheduled for completion within 27 months.

Now, this is close to home: once upon a time there was a pleasant water meadow upon which cattle grazed between the River Aire and what became Wellington Street. Then along came one Benjamin Gott, in 1742, who built a mill on the site which was to push Leeds into the forefront of the Industrial Revolution and secure for the city the leadership of the 19th-century woollen trade. He gave his project the name Bean Ing Mill and it revolutionised the former cottage industry by using machinery and large-scale factory production. It also set him on the road to fame and fortune. And why is it close to home? Bean Ing Mill seen here in the process of being demolished in January 1965, made way for the erection of the Yorkshire Post Newspapers Building which has pioneered the used of advanced newspaper technology since it came into use in September 1970.

The fascinating big bang you are about to witness (in your imagination) did not come about as a result of a bout of 'phone rage' generated by a disgruntled British Telecom customer. The fact is that BT simply wanted rid of Telecom House which stood, on rather spindly legs many thought, on a site overlooking the Inner Ring Road, Westgate, Park Lane road complex. This picture shows how it looked shortly before the demolition men went into action. Homes in the area were cleared of residents, and major roads in the vicinity were closed that Sunday morning. Experts employed by the Controlled Demolition Group Ltd., placed (need it be said 'carefully') 1,250 explosive charges. Then the crowd, made-up of 'Loiners' from all over Leeds, fell silent…

At 10.30am – precisely – 12-year-old Suzie Pratt, of The Nooks, Gildersome, near Leeds, whose name had been picked out of a hat, triggered off the blast. A mighty cheer went up as the landmark building shivered, and then started to cave in.

Pictured here when it was about halfway down, the building started to shower glass over nearby roads, then clouds of smoke and dust rose into the air as – from this vantage point – the International Pool emerged into view for the first time in years (see the last picture in the 'Ever Changing City Section' for that full view; and the huge roundabout which was positioned just about where the smoking remains of Telecom House are piled up in the foreground of the next picture).

When the dust settled, there seemed to be surprisingly little rubble. But then, the building was nearly all glass-walled; and it would need a lot of open space to absorb all that hot air from those people who find it nice to talk – at length.

Parks a-plenty

Under the heading 'The 'Lungs' of a City', pictures and text in *Memory Lane, Leeds 1*, which highlighted the city's parks raised enough interest to merit more space being devoted to this subject. This extract from the *Yorkshire Post* of 5 October 1871, reveals how one of the best-known parks in the north of England was purchased: a deal which the citizens of Leeds have had cause to bless for well over a century...

opening address in the Mechanics' Insti vote of thanks was afterwards accorded to the motion of the MAYOR OF LEEDS, seconded LAKE. The various departments meet to-day rooms at the Town Hall.

THE new order for the reduction of on inland letters will take effect to-day. A let exceeding 1 oz. not exceeding 2 o and so on to 12 oz. for 4d.

THE Roundhay Park estate was offered for sale, and the MAYOR, representin Corporation of Leeds, in accordance with the d of the Council and a public meeting of rate became the purchaser of the mansion and pl grounds, including the lakes, for £107,000. bought Lot 20, by which an entrance to the pa be provided half a mile nearer Leeds than the p entrance. For this lot £32,000 was given, makin total sum expended £139,000. Of the forty-five offered, 28 were sold, the total sum realised £170,545. The remaining 17 lots were withdraw

BY an explosion of fire damp in one o pits in the Aberdare Valley yesterday, five men killed and others severely injured.

Some interesting examples of contraptions for transporting infants (the wheelbarrow belonged to the gardener), appear in this 1900 view of Burley Park. What is not clear is whether it was spring or autumn, but despite the bright sunlight, there was a general atmosphere of the children being told to "get well-wrapped up".

Now here's a name to raise eyebrows and cause puzzled looks to appear upon the majority of 'Loiners's' faces when they are asked if they know the location of Charley Cake Park. As the author found, if they live north of the river, the majority will shake their heads. If they come from the area around Armley, there's a fair chance that (a) they have heard of it but can't place it; or (b) know that bits of it still exist and can just about describe where they are.

Tracing its history proved difficult; establishing how it got its name – near impossible – although the general opinion is that a chap named Charley made cakes and sold them to visitors to the park. Though faded, this picture gives some clues as to its location. The road coming up from the left of this 'V' site had a tram line and, indeed, an open-topped electric tram can be seen at the far end of the line of bushes.

So, claim the locals, the section of Charley Cake Park in this picture was at the junction of Town Street, Armley, and Whingate. It was obviously kept in good order and that must have been a blessing for the residents of the houses across the road.

The 'castle' in Roundhay Park was not one of the homes 'that Cromwell knocked abaht a bit,' as the old ditty went. Twentieth-century vandals were mainly responsible for the knocked about appearance of this once substantial structure.

Generations of children have woven fantasies about its past but, regrettably, it can boast no history of dragons, knights chasing fair maidens (or vice-versa). In fact it was a 'folly' or phoney castle, believed to have been built more for use as a summer house than a fort to repel louts from Lancashire.

Its builders were almost certainly members of the Nicholson family, who were the last private owners of Roundhay Park; and its construction is believed to have coincided with the creation of Waterloo Lake around 1821.

Unfortunately, not all the children, nor some of their older brethren visiting the 'castle' were living in fantasy land, and even this substantially-built edifice began to crumble at the hands, and feet, of climbing children and moronic vandals. But as the song goes… 'the Rockies may crumble…' and the 'castle' began to go the same way. However, as this small girl's thoughts were probably with the past as she wandered down the well-worn path past its towers, with wild flowers everywhere and she thinking of knights in armour serenading their ladies; well, just maybe as the song also goes, her 'love was here to stay…'

Hey! don't you know there's a war on? That question, beloved of air raid wardens who found a squint of light on the edge of someone's black-out curtains in World War Two, springs to mind at the sight of these goings-on at Roundhay Park's bathing and paddling pools on Whit Monday, 1944.

But the sun was shining and there was a glimmer of light at the end of the wartime tunnel, revealing that the Allies were gaining the upper hand on most fronts and the green, green fields of peace might just be on the horizon. Certainly, if a German bomber pilot had parachuted into the middle of this lot, they would have more likely thrown him in the pool with a sense of fun than a desire to do him any real harm – for that was Yorkshire folk all over.

Roundhay Park had not been open to the public long before it became a favourite place for Sunday walks and evening strolls. The Edwardians delighted in its wide open spaces after the hustle and bustle of doing business in the city centre, although there certainly seemed to be more trees around the park in those days.

The sounds of things to come shattered the customary peace of Roundhay on Saturday, 19 October 1929, when for the first time the Northern Motor Boat Club held a series of speedboat races on Waterloo Lake. Thousands of spectators lined the lake when five races, each of four miles, were held and speeds of up to 40mph were reached. However, veteran local residents, some 60 years later, now claim that the decibel rating of the speed boats has been exceeded by participants in recent pop concerts at this great open-air venue.

A firm favourite with the younger set, this 'Spirit of the Woods' statue was found on the Fulham, London, premises of Crowthers – specialists in antique garden ornaments, and brought to Roundhay by Mr L. G. Knight, the then Leeds Director of Parks. It was a firm favourite as a background for photographs of toddlers trying to identify the woodland creatures – including rabbits, frogs, mice and various birds – sculptured around the base by its originator – G. W. Ashmore.

But all that joy turned to horror on Christmas morning, 1957, when those out for a head-clearing stroll found that both arms had been removed from the statue some time on Christmas Eve by vandals over-filled with what some like to call the Christmas spirit. That the act was deliberate was confirmed when a search led to the recovery of the two arms from nearby shrubbery; one had been sawn off. Fortunately, an expert decided they could be restored to the statue without it being disfigured.

"I say, chaps – what about a jolly old spin round the park on our bikes?" No luminous lycra gear for this upstanding velocipede rider as he poses for the photographer at the edge of the lake at East End Park in the early 1900s. As for the crush of children on the seats; either the chap on the extreme right of the right-hand bench had a very large family, or this was some kind of school outing. Note that sweeping, tree-lined boulevard on the extreme right, then take that house out of the picture and this might well have been somewhere in La Belle France.

For all that we have seen and heard of pop concerts in Leeds parks in the last 20 years, none has had quite such an attractive setting as this band stand in its own open air amphitheatre in Western Flatts Park, Wortley, many years ago. And having witnessed a huge rock concert in a setting very similar to this in Sydney not all that long ago, the author reckons such a location offers food for thought for developers eager to put Leeds in a much higher position in today's entertainment business.

Whatever Roundhay had in terms of a conventional park, if 'Loiners' – and people from towns for miles around – wanted a day out in the country, in a park which boasted some attractions that were to be developed out of all recognition in later years by the huge American amusement parks, they went to Golden Acre: just off the main Leeds-Otley Road near Bramhope.

In its lifetime, from the early 1930s to 1939, it attracted countless thousands. One of its main attractions was its large lake, which still exists, but considerably reduced in size. Twice in its lifetime the lake came into the world of aviation; firstly around 1934 when, as pictured in this rather faint print, it hosted the Supermarine S5 Seaplane which had been the winner of a Schneider Trophy Race. Secondly, it was drained in World War Two so as not to provide a guide on moonlight nights for German bombers trying to find the giant Avro factory at nearby Yeadon, where Lancaster bombers were to become its most famous product.

Reminiscent of certain areas of Scarborough's Peasholm Park, this 1982 view within the bounds of Golden Acre shows why so many people continue to visit the site today. A credit to the Parks Department who use the site for plant trials, it is also home to many forms of wildlife; and being within little over 20 minutes from the city centre, forms the perfect escape from the hustle and bustle of downtown.

The heyday of gracious living in Potternewton is no better illustrated than by this view of the ivy-covered mansion, and its gardens which had been laid-out with some considerable thought by the original owners. It stands in Potternewton Park, which was acquired by Leeds City Council in 1902, and the purchase of an additional piece of land in 1923 meant the public were eventually free to roam the 100 or so grassy acres at will – and go right up to the very doors of the mansion. Today, however, it is fenced-off from the main park and used as a further education centre. Picture from Mrs L. Donohue, Glensdale Street, Leeds 9.

Less well-known than Golden Acre, but nevertheless a wide-open space well worth investigating – being not much more than a six-hit from the Headingley Ground – Beckett Park has long been overshadowed by its neighbour's fame, generated by cricket and rugby. Those who take the trouble to walk through its acres will, if persistent, find this gem, now almost hidden away at the end of an avenue of trees, once known as Queen's Walk where the surrounding vegetation has almost hidden the arch which once stood proud in the city centre.

It was originally erected to mark the visit to Leeds by Queen Victoria on 7 September 1858, for the inauguration of the Town Hall – information which is recorded in the strips between the arch and the top of its supporting stone columns. Popular theory at the time was that the Queen was to have her first view of Leeds from the arch; what was not taken into consideration was that she would have been facing in the wrong direction.

Some of their opponents were moved to suggest that the worthy aldermen responsible for its sighting probably preferred it that way, considering the state of mid-nineteenth century Leeds in the immediate vicinity!

Disfigured by graffiti, and suffering from deterioration, the arch was restored in October 1984, on behalf of the Leeds Society of Architects. It seems sad that it should be hidden away on the fringe of the Beckett Park Campus – dismissed, in effect, as is Queen Victoria's plinth-mounted statue which once graced the front of the Town Hall, but which was banished to Woodhouse Moor years ago. It, too, became a target for graffiti merchants…

The Quarry Hill saga

On 28 March 1938, the *Yorkshire Post* carried a story which began: 'The Leeds Director of Housing, Mr R. A. H. Livett, peered inquisitively into a big hole in a scullery sink. "That's where the rubbish will go," he said. "There is a gauge which will not allow you to put anything too big down the hole, but it will accommodate tins, bottles and other normal household refuse." The device could also be used as a normal sink.'

Mr Livett was explaining the wonders of what was to become a world-famous block of flats – Quarry Hill – of which the Lord Mayor, Mr J. Badlay, was to open the first section (40 of the total 938 flats) two days later. They were designed by Mr Livett in consultation with a French engineer, Mr N. E. Mopin. Built by Tarran Industries, the total cost was around £600,000, which at today's prices would get you about six so-called 'executive houses'.

Work commenced on the project in 1936 with, initially, five flats being completed each day – thanks to the Mopin method of mass production. There were mixed feelings about the new 'wonder sinks' – but people soon got used to them, and folks tussling with wheelie bins and plastic bags on a freezing winter's day in Mr Blair's thoroughly modern Britain, might well think the 'ancients' of 60 years ago had some better ideas.

Claimed to be the biggest block of flats in Europe, housing some 3,000 people on a 23-acre site, Quarry Hill was a wonderland to families moved there from slum areas of the city. There were 88 lifts and staircases were lit by electricity controlled by clock meters.

A *YEP* reporter, wrote of 'sun porches, a basement area reserved for prams, cycles, hawkers' barrows and trim little window boxes. Outside it is possible to visualise the wonderful layout of the gardens, recreation areas and the streets of this town in miniature.'

In due course the Quarry Hill Tenants Association was formed. There was a Social Theatre with its own *Children's Hour* to rival that broadcast by the BBC and lots, lots more

going on. Unhappily, this included murders; and the lengthy search for an ingenious 'flasher', whose 'trousers', beneath his raincoat, only extended from his shoe tops to just above his knees, allowing him to escape detection even when in the close proximity of detectives!

However, serious construction faults were discovered when the flats were little more than 20 years old, and in 1961 much of the steelwork was found to be corroded. Some £500,000 was spent on giving the flats a further ten years' life; after which it was estimated that another £1.5 million would be needed to keep them standing and fit for habitation.

A *YEP* headline of later years: 'Half dream, half nightmare – but always in the news' summed-up the action-filled but comparatively short lifespan of Quarry Hill. On 18 August 1975, demolition began and, as the saying goes – the rest is history; with the site of the flats almost as clear as it had been two or three years before the sink inspectors arrived in 1938…

In the early 1700s, Quarry Hill was still quite pleasant meadowland, rising gently towards Richmond Hill and Burmantofts. By January 1936, when the picture on this rather battered print was taken, the well-known trade marks of the industrial revolution had obliterated any green and pleasant land. The small cottages which remained had been crowded-in by factories, small businesses, and the onward march of Leeds's famous terraces.

Never mind the work going ahead on the flats in the background; the assortment of fascinating vehicles in this 1936-37 view is enough to give the average vintage vehicle enthusiast the vapours. The cars included splendid Morris, Austin, Riley, Wolseley and Ford models. The American import on the famous Appleyard of Leeds island site filling station was probably taking more fuel on board than any three of the other cars could hold; after all, it was almost as big as the petrol tanker alongside. That wonderful old double-decker passing what would become an entrance to Quarry Hill flats, on the left, had one of those trench-like gangways on the upper deck that would often be lost in a smokers' fog. The driver of the Albion lorry on the extreme right was no doubt quietly cursing the old moke, its rear quarters kindly covered with an old blanket, pulling the coal cart in front. Yet in those days road rage was unknown. It was more often a case of "After you, Claude…" "No, after you Cecil…" as drivers remembered their manners!

Some idea of the rapid progress made using the Mopin method of mass production can be gained from this aerial view of the site, also taken around 1936-37. The long production sheds in which some of the pre-fabricated work was prepared are on the right, alongside Marsh Lane. This picture gives a good impression of how the system worked, from the seemingly delicate tracery of the steelwork near the gas-holder, to the part-fronted flats in front of the church, then on to the near-completed blocks in the corner between Marsh Lane and New York Road. The main Leeds-York railway line curves across the bottom right-hand corner of the picture.

And here were some of the lads who made it all possible. An article in the *YEP* during the 1980s recalled the way in which lunchtime crowds would gather to watch the workers on the Quarry Hill project. One of those workers was Mr John Lunn who laboured on the production of concrete slabs, having travelled to Leeds seeking work after his previous job as a Hull trawlerman was lost owing to the shortage of work.

His wife, Mrs Lily Lunn sent this picture to the editor of the *YEP*, explaining that she took it of her husband, sitting third from the left, with fellow

workers on the Quarry Hill project. The arch which became the main entrance to the flats is on the right. Later on, John worked on another Leeds project – the excavations for Lewis's store.

The Lunns were married on Christmas Day, 1936. John's brother, George, then still working as a Hull trawlerman, could only get Christmas Day off to be best man; hence the choice of date. A chocolate yule log formed the table centrepiece at the reception. George asked if he could take the remains of it back to share with his shipmates.

Sadly, he was drowned whilst on Russian convoy duty in 1942 and following that the Lunns always had a commemorative yule log on Christmas Day. In today's crazy world, one wonders if such sacrifices by 'westerners' are marked in any way by the Russians…

Reference was made in the introduction to this section of the costs involved in up-grading, refurbishing – call it what you will – of the flats over the years. This photograph shows the section facing the bottom of Eastgate following their 'rejuvenation' in the mid-1960s. Appleyard's famous island site petrol station on the right, was incidentally, claimed to be the only such station on a roundabout in Britain. On the left, work is going on – 'yet again' some would say – on deepening and widening the infamous Sheepscar Beck, whose progress to this point from its start near Otley Chevin is referred to elsewhere in this publication. This work was carried-out before another set of major changes saw the second roundabout – in the background – replaced by a New York Road flyover.

The New York Road flyover referred to in the caption with the previous picture, can be seen here crossing the Eastgate-Regent Street connection when the work on the 'all-American' section of the flyover and slip-road-equipped New York Road was completed. This pristine memory-provoking aerial picture is probably one of the best taken of the Quarry Hill complex before Messrs Livett and Mopin's brain child bit the dust and the whole process of development around Quarry Hill began again, leading toward such delights as the DHSS Headquarters (nick-named 'The Chinese Embassy') and the Leeds Playhouse.

Whatever else, Livett and Mopin's great plan proved two things: it was amazing what Quarry Hill residents could get down their sinks and, more seriously and importantly, it lifted thousands of slum dwellers into a safer, softer, much-appreciated environment. Six years after the first 1,000 families moved in, the Leeds MOH announced that the child mortality rate in the complex was only 10.9 per thousand, compared with 13.4 for the rest of Leeds.

That area of pleasant meadow land, rising gently toward Richmond Hill and Burmantofts in the 1700s – as described in the first caption in this section – lay under all that you see on the left of this picture, which was published the day after Leeds City Council decided, in 1971, to demolish the flats. At a stroke, some 3,000 people – most of whom had been lifted from the slums to new heights of what was then modern living – were faced with leaving behind what had proved to be one of the most daring housing experiments in Europe, if not the world. It had its faults, yes, but it also generated enough that was good for health and happiness to persuade local authorities from Brooklyn to Berlin, Chicago to Shanghai, that the scourge of slums could, and would, be tackled.

As the 1970s wore on, the demolition men and their mighty machines moved on to the Quarry Hill site and this example of the latter was ideally positioned to look as if it was going to bite a chunk out a section of the flats. The bulldozers bit-off not only concrete and steel; they rampaged through areas where thousands of people had been given a better chance in life; had made countless friends – and a few enemies, one assumes – but the close-knit community that made up Quarry Hill was in the main of decent folk and one feels that whatever future redevelopments pile one upon the other, those former residents who revisit the site to point it out to grandchildren and great-grandchildren (as many already do) will, in general, be happy with the memory that they were a part of a great social experiment.

"Ee 'arry, why did 'ter go an' pull that lever that said do not touch – now see what tha's done!" You can imagine such banter, and a few more ribald remarks about "that lass still in the bathroom of one of them flats on't third floor…" and so on as this picture was being taken, in 1978, of one of the demolition teams framed by what had been one of the entrance arches to the flats. Note the spindle-like twisted girders, in the foreground; then study those still in place in the next picture.

Readers in the construction business might well have taken several close looks at these photographs of the steel framing that went into the Quarry Hill blocks and wondered… On the other hand, perhaps the secret of Livett and Mopin's construction techniques lay in the way these part-pre-fabricated buildings were put together.

By the time they reached the end of the line stage pictured here, in June 1978, one could be forgiven for thinking that it was a scene more reminiscent of several blitzed European cities at the end of World War Two, rather than the end of a (some would say arguably) worthwhile experiment to give people a better standard of living.

Bridges spanning the years

With so many of the world's great cities located on rivers, the bridges built to cross them spring easily to mind and no publicity brochure worth its salt fails to picture one or two of them. Although Leeds literally began where the first Leeds Bridge was erected across the River Aire; and by the subsequent naming of the then premier street Briggate; that bridge's location was always easy to describe; subsequent crossings tended to be essential workaday structures rather than outstanding works of art or design; but in recent years there have been substantial improvements. This renovation work and successful attempts to make the bridges more appealing to the eye have resulted in their greater prominence. Let's take an imaginary journey downstream from Kirkstall.

Although not strictly a bridge, Kirkstall Viaduct, pictured here, commands a good deal of attention as it makes its great sweep across the valley.

Taken in March 1991, this photograph showed the earlier cleaning-up to remove years of Leeds industrial by-products had certainly made it more presentable.

The viaduct was built to allow the Leeds and Thirsk Railway to gain a reasonably level crossing of the River Aire from the heights of Armley to the point where trains could start the long climb from Burley, through Headingley and Horsforth to Cookridge, before plunging into Bramhope Tunnel for the descent into Wharfedale.

What a pity, therefore, that in its plans to ease road congestion on this main artery – Kirkstall Road – into and out of the city, the powers that be did not see fit, years ago, to take advantage of the sensibly wide arches of the viaduct to line-up a dual carriageway all the way from where the Inner Ring Road flyover now stands to the Kirkstall Lights crossroads…

Following-on that last observation, it might be hard for a visitor to envisage that one of the city's most important central highways carries its thundering traffic below this, not so old as you might think, hump-backed bridge over the Inner Ring Road near St George's Church. Back in 1989, when this picture was taken, the Leeds Civic Trust alleged that the bridge gave a 'deplorable impression' of the city because of 'its bad state and design'. In a letter to the Leeds City Council's Highways, Engineering and Cleansing Services Committee, the Trust drew attention to the unsatisfactory condition of the bridge linking Great George Street with Woodhouse Square. But no doubt the locals would have preferred any sort of condition rather than the long walk round which would have been necessary had not the bridge been built.

Ask anyone in Boar Lane how to get to Neville Street and if they know anything of the city centre at all, they will invariably say: "Turn left at City Square and go down under the Dark Arches…" That's fair enough – and it certainly used to be pretty dark and gloomy under the railway viaduct – for that is what they really meant – which made up part of Leeds City Station. The real dark arches began west of the station where the locks, sluices,

weirs and tunnels of River Aire and the Aire and Calder Navigation Canal mingled with the cat's cradle of railway lines in that area. Here a train is crossing arches dark enough to require electric lights inside them even in daylight hours.

It could be the opening sequence for some British film shot – almost as ever – in London. In fact this was a view of the cleaned-up Victoria Bridge, in Neville Street, – now in the midst of a whole range of riverside developments where some of the 'London set', transferred to jobs in Leeds, have already taken-up residence in what is rapidly-becoming a desirable area of the city in which to live.

What it says about the desirability of riverside residences in the previous caption could hardly have been imagined when this picture was taken on 15 March 1967. The photographer was just upstream from Leeds Bridge, with a clutter of old warehouses in the distance. Similar buildings are on the right but some new construction is underway on the left (north) side of the river where there was a parking area for Leeds City Transport buses. (How many readers can remember the art of running and jumping on; or dropping off those open platforms when the buses were in motion?)

This particular parking spot was on the site of the King's Mill where, for centuries, 'Loiners' had ground their corn. A carved stone panel on the riverside wall bore the name of the mill. 'New proposals mean this site could become a pleasant riverside precinct,' said a part of the original caption on the photo. It was an accurate forecast, for most of this area has been cleaned-up; there are plush flats in many of the redeveloped warehouses and one of the city's top hotels stands on a site just beyond the bridge.

Those who could recall the Leeds waterfront in the worst days of its pollution and decay were among the first to hail the enormous clean-up operations which have now been going on for some years; also the large amount of development – especially south of the river. This view of Crown Point Bridge could easily have fooled some people into believing it was somewhere south of Watford; or even on the Continent.

The photograph was taken in September 1988, at a time when Leeds City Council highways officers were carrying out the paperwork needed for a ban on lorries weighing over 17 tons because the bridge was getting too old to take the strain. Perhaps now is the time to suggest that a similar ban be imposed on heavy lorries which are turning the country roads on the fringes of the north side of the city into 'rat runs' and causing enormous damage to the edges of those roads, ditch supports, verges, hedgerows and wildlife in the process...

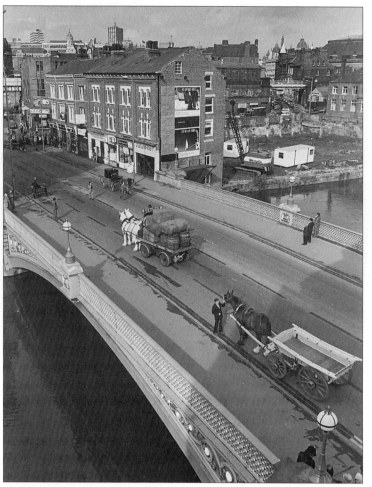

The start of the city's 1988 film festival was marked by some 'period' film making on Leeds Bridge itself, where double yellow lines and other road markings were blacked-out so as not to spoil the effect of the horse-drawn traffic. What the producer and director said about the 20th-century street lamps, advertisement hoardings and suchlike is not known; they must also have muttered abut the rubber tyres on two of the carts. Still, that's no worse than the tyre tracks left by speeding camera trucks filming the US Cavalry chasing Indians in many a western movie; and certainly no worse than one of Geronimo's 'warriors' wearing a wrist-watch… But you have to admit that Leeds Bridge itself made a star appearance in this shot. Picture: Jack Hickes Photographers Ltd.

This was probably the largest and heaviest steel bridge structure in the city and brings to an end our journey downstream which began at Kirkstall. The only thing which remains of this massive piece of late 19th-century engineering, that used to be a feature of south-east Leeds, is the massive stone load-bearing tower in the foreground. The bridge was built at Thwaite Gate to carry the Great Northern Railway line from Beeston Junction (near the top of Dewsbury Road), over the Aire and Calder Navigation Canal to Hunslet East Goods station.

About that time, rumour had it that the Aire & Calder intended to establish a Yorkshire version of the Manchester Ship Canal linking the East Coast with Leeds. The GN, meanwhile, had planned its link to cross both the River Aire and the canal at this point. On learning that the canal company planned to operate much taller ships, the GN decided on a swing bridge of massive proportions and this was the result.

It proved to be a costly gamble for the GN. On its first (and only) trials, the far end of the bridge seen in this picture failed to lock back into position at the proper level; possibly because the structure was over-weight. Repeated attempts failed to get the running rails to line-up with the fixed lines and, in due course, the 'swinging' part of the operation was abandoned.

Ironically – tongue in cheek one suspects – the Aire and Calder Navigation then announced they were not going to operate tall ships… The fixed bridge continued in use for some time but was demolished in the 1970s.

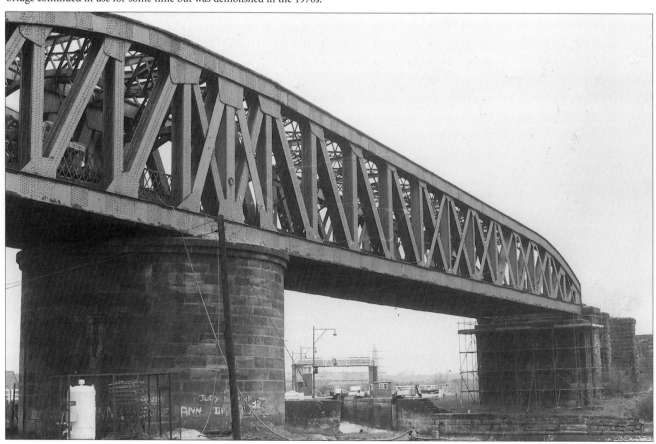

Some Transports
of Delight

There can be little to add about transport in Leeds to what was said under that heading in *Memory Lane, Leeds 1.* In the three short years since that edition was published work has started on the refurbishment of the city's main railway station – with benefits for passengers within the station itself; and for them and the people who have to operate the trains, through the sorting-out of the notorious bottle-neck of lines to the west of the station.

On the roads, work on the new City Centre Loop has been pretty well completed; although not exactly to the satisfaction of many drivers who say it drives them loopy and they find access to premises within its circle is about as easy as breeching some the better-made medieval fortresses.

As for the long-proposed Supertram well, it has been a long time coming and still hasn't arrived – and more down-to-earth transport enthusiasts question the need for a futuristic-looking streamlined train snaking through the streets when a system of more straight-forward, multiple-unit trams, fitted with modern comforts and safeguards – as used in a number of European cities – might make more sense.

For one thing, single cars can be run in quiet periods whilst others can be added – up to several units – as and when there is a bigger demand from passengers.

These Continental cities do not, it seems, suffer from the onslaughts of British bogeymen who persist in saying that such systems hold-up other road traffic. It could be suggested that the problem here is over-control of traffic via a deluge of painted instructions, and a forest of 'street furniture', as bigger hazards to smooth traffic operation.

A railway centre

Though not exactly a Crewe in terms of main line importance linked with railway equipment manufacturing works; Leeds came near to that level in the growth years of the railways and, as a crossroads on the national rail system, there was little to choose in terms of importance between it and the Cheshire rail centre.

Lines literally ran in all directions to and from Leeds, with the heaviest concentration in the south-west segment. Various operating companies were keen to establish stations as near the city centre as possible, but the take-up of land through the rapid development of factories and domestic premises in the 1800s meant some companies had to settle for shared running on lines approaching and within the city and, consequently, stations also got mixed usage.

As times went on, there was an obvious need for a more prestigious main station and amalgamations and sharing led, in due course, to the building of this magnificent 'North Concourse', pictured on 3 January 1939 at the then Leeds City Station. It owed something of its design to the magnificent 'Union' stations located in a number of American cities, where several railroads benefited from a common central station. Not least, its 'gate' system of entry to various platforms was a replica of an idea the US railroads had borrowed from the airlines; or vice-versa.

The North Concourse became a sad sight in the past decade when it twas reduced to use as a car park, but new developments are bringing back that old sparkle and, it is expected, a station of which Leeds can again be proud.

That sad sight can be appreciated from this picture of 23 April 1985. At that stage the future of the concourse was in the balance. The then owners of the Queens Hotel wanted to turn it into an exclusive car park for its customers; but Leeds planners opposed the move because they were considering better things which, it turned-out, are coming to fruition.

The folly of a certain Prime Minister regularly going on about 'modernising Britain' is no better illustrated than by this picture of the Wellington Street entrance to the North Concourse. This picture was taken in later years but, in fact, it is how it looked when the concourse first opened, before World War Two. The 'flying saucer' design would not look out of place as an entrance to one of Mr Blair's favourite projects – the Millennium Dome – put up some 60 years after this Leeds structure!

All that remains of a famous enterprise: this sad-looking bridge across the River Aire, just east of the Yorkshire Post Newspapers Building in Wellington Street, is all that remains of the main lines into Central Station: the starting point for most of the 'crack' Leeds expresses to London. The space on the bridge carrying the lines on which streamlined A4 locomotives of the LNER, many with names that were famous the world over, pulled trains in and out is now a tangle of weeds, grass and bushes between artistic balustrades which are gradually being demolished by mindless vandals. If ever the city council gets around to developing a parkland strip alongside these river banks, the bridge should be cleaned-up and restored to its former glory; for it is a stylish reminder that it was a part of the historic infrastructure which put Leeds on the world's big business map.

As announced by a notice on the wall in the foreground, this was the station approach to the Central Station from Wellington Street; with a rather jumbled set of architectural styles represented on the main frontage up above. The rather tatty name board on the roof did little for what was an important station, which in terms of business travellers in particular, probably generated far more first-class tickets than did City Station: which is probably why Moss Bros. – the top people's tailors, had a prominent poster on the wall.

The hairstyles and fashions of the young ladies in this photograph – taken on 30 July 1966, certainly recall the heyday of some British pop stars. The picture also underlines the old adage that when the British go on holiday, even in July, many dress to face all weathers. It was taken on the concourse at the Wellington Street end of Central's platforms.

The great expresses which shuttled between Central Station and King's Cross are probably remembered best for the famed steam engines, particularly Sir Nigel Gresley's A4 Class streamliners. But in terms of efficiency and speed, the 'Deltic' Class of large and powerful diesels were hard to beat. Only 22 were built for BR but their 3,300hp Napier engines provided world-beating reliability. One of them – No.9010 *The King's Own Scottish Borderer*, clocked-up a world record in January 1973, by completing two million miles in revenue earning service in just under 12 years.

The East Coast Main Line was their scene, but they did get into Leeds, too, and this one is pictured entering Central – a treat for the local spotters. Incidentally, the stone structure on the left was one of two wagon-lifting towers which stood in the goods yard alongside the station, at Wellington Street level. This one had a water tank on its roof (also see another view in this section).

Central Station had served the community well, but times were a'changing and in its last days the place took on a sad and forlorn appearance; as this picture of 11 November 1962 clearly shows. In its final years, sections of the train shed roof badly-needed repair and/or replacement and, of course, with the demise of steam power, the long open vents above the tracks, through which steam and smoke were exhausted, were no longer necessary (nor was the wind, rain and snow they let in, said many a passenger). And, so as services were transferred to Leeds City, the station which had long echoed the haunting wails of A4 Pacific whistles as they set out for London's bright lights, came to the end of its career and the demolition men moved in...

What most passengers never realised was that the Central Station complex was a major feat of construction, for practically all of it north of that still remaining bridge across over the River Aire, was built up above the water meadows which formerly ran down to the river. This meant that nearly all the stonework involved (and some of it was massive), had to be brought in via the new line; so had all the earth and rubble fill used among the maze of arches built to carry the station and its lines.

Some of the stonework in the support and retaining walls which carried the lines over Northern Street, between Whitehall Road and Wellington Street, was so massive that it was left *in situ* when the station was demolished. Some idea of the size of the structure can be gained from the estimate that its platforms were about on a level with the third floor of the Royal Mail building which was subsequently erected on the station site.

Most of those arches under the station approach (as in this picture), were rented by small, private companies engaged in all manner of businesses. Most of the rest of the former meadow area was occupied by a railway goods yard, transshipment sheds and warehouses, and a block of offices which faced on to Wellington Street.

The wall of that block was scarred by bomb fragments from a World War Two air-raid, as is the large wall – still standing – which divided the goods yard from the remains of the former Bean Ing Mill site; now the location of the Yorkshire Post Newspapers Building.

This wagon lift tower, mentioned earlier, was felt worthy of preservation and still stands in the Aireside Centre – the name given to the shopping and warehouse complex which fills much of the old station area. In this view, the level of the railway lines above the arches can clearly be seen – it runs across the bottom of the two open arched wagon exits. Various suggestions have been made and plans discussed for the future use of the tower, but none have come to fruition.

Leaving Central Station behind, we travel eastward – as the old cinema travelogues used to say – though not by a line from Central; and find ourselves amid the goings-on at Crossgates station. This busy suburb, which provides a large amount of commuter traffic for the railway, was a mere village outside Leeds when the Leeds and Selby Railway opened in 1834. But the fact that it was on the route of the new line led, without doubt, to its rapid growth and prosperity. Note the clerestory roofed coaches, equipped with running boards; and some magnificent gas lanterns under the canopy on the left.

This print gives a better view of the gas lights and also of the smartly turned-out station staff, who obviously took pride in their floral displays around 1914. There's a poster advertising excursions to Tynemouth, and looking further along the platform it is easy to see that everyone knew their place: there was a Ladies' Room (Third Class); Gentlemen's Room (First Class) and a General Room. What facilities there were for Third Class male passengers isn't clear. But let's hope they acted as gentlemen and respected the end-of-platform flower tub on cold nights…

And finally, this railway section comes to a close with the scene on the day Crossgates station said goodbye to its gas-lamps, one of which is pictured, after 68 years' service. Electricity – that bane of the gas mantle manufacturer, finally arrived at Crossgates in the early 1970s. The station had been built in the early days of the Leeds and Selby Railway but it was 1902, when its buildings were 'modernised' (Mr Blair please note), that gas lighting was first introduced. And it remained in use longer than at almost any other station in the country. One reason, perhaps, was that Crossgate's residents using the station found it not only a pleasant link with the past; but also something they looked forward to seeing on winter evenings.

The coming of the car

Faced with a 'drivers from hell' situation several times a day – at least, that's how many a motorist sees 50 per cent of other drivers on the road these days – most of them would be hard put to imagine, or recall, just how 'open' conditions were in the old days, and the joys, of 'the open road'.

The fact that even in the 1960s, it was possible to drive for several miles on many a Yorkshire road and never see another vehicle, seems unbelievable to today's 'go faster' generation; constantly frustrated by the fact that it takes longer and longer to travel even short distances, than it did but a few years ago.

Despite all, the average motorist would, it seems, prefer to put up with it all than go without his, or her, car. For whether you want to show off in it; flash around in it, clean it after every time you have taken it out, or fling stuff all over it until it looks and smells like a mobile dustbin (don't kid yourself there are no drivers like that), it may take unimaginable pressures to finally force them on to public transport.

In the meantime, let's take a look at how we got here (or where we're coming from, in today's jargon); and being the gentlemen we are, we'll give this lady the honour of pole position in this collection of pictures.

As can be seen by the number plate, U10 was the tenth motor vehicle to be registered in Leeds. Believed to be a Renault, it belonged to Mr James Parker, a fruit and veg. trader in Kirkgate Market. The picture came to the *YEP* from Mr John Parker, of Bradford, who explained that the lady in the car was Mrs James Parker who originally sent it to her niece, Maud, around 1905. It still bears the message: 'With Aunty's Love.' It seems unlikely that Mrs Parker would have driven the car; more likely that she climbed aboard to pose for the picture. Even so, she looks petrified at the thought that this horseless carriage thing might leap forward and carry her off to heaven only knows where. Mr John Parker, was the great-nephew of James, and says he came from the Bradford side of the family and never knew the Leeds Parkers. Well that's that, then.

Of the same vintage as the car in the previous picture, this two-cylinder Rolls-Royce was found scrapped at a farm on the outskirts of Leeds by the late Oliver Langton, of Horsforth – a famous name in northern motoring circles. He spent five years rebuilding the Rolls and, pictured here with its U44 plate, was one of the most rare cars among 321 pre-1905 vehicles taking part in the annual RAC London to Brighton Run on Sunday, 4 November 1955; which was about the time this photograph was taken.

Another Langton, Eric in this case, took three years to rebuild this 1906 N Model Ford, pictured at a garage in Water Lane where it was on display to the public. The vehicle cost 500 US dollars when originally purchased and was worth over £8,000 by the time Eric's handiwork had it looking almost as new.

Mr Peter Black, well-known throughout Yorkshire for his interest in vintage vehicles, turned up at the 1967 Pudsey Show in this splendidly-restored, 60-year-old French-built Niclausse and swept the lady fans (of cars, of course) off their feet.

Miss Christine Morris, then 24 and a Sheffield teacher, just didn't have enough spare cash on her to buy this 1907 Renault when it appeared at an auction sale of vintage and veteran cars at Rothwell, Leeds, in March 1970. "If you had a ride in that, you'd really feel like a lady," she sighed, making eyes at her accompanying boyfriend who was a veteran car enthusiast, but didn't have enough cash on him to even make a start in the bidding. And so this beautiful star of the show (the car) went unsold. Wonder where it is today?

From beauty to the beast: back in 1910, this sturdy lorry was a familiar sight on the streets of Leeds with driver Jim Hall and his mate Lewis Grimshaw on board. And it was a bit of a grim carry on, too, with no cabin for shelter and wheels with solid tyres almost shaking your teeth out as they bounced over the cobbles. The photograph was taken in Dewsbury Road where the posters proclaimed that Clarice Mayne was appearing in the pantomime *Dick Whittington*, although we can't see at which theatre; and Animated Pictures were showing elsewhere. "Bah, gum, Lewis, ah could do wi' a pint." "Aye, me an' all, Jim. 'Appen this chap tekkin us likenesses will buy us one?" "Aye, an' 'appen not…" If he was a *YEP* photographer, he almost certainly did. Yer wot?

Now this is something – no solid tyres here, old chap, this set-up just reeks of better things. Mr H. R. Kirk, a pioneer Leeds motorist, was at the wheel of this superb 1910 Mercedes with Mr Reg Smith as his companion. The machine was equipped with chain drive, acetylene lamps and pneumatic (blow up) tyres. The pair seem to be dressed for a drive across the Russian Steppes and the young Mr Smith might have had some concern regarding Mr Kirk's driving skills, for the position of his feet at right angles to the minute running board ahead of the driving sprocket indicate that he was prepared to make a rapid exit if necessary. The 'Merc' was certainly ahead of its time – note the bulb horn in the centre of the steering wheel. Or was it there to act as an early model air bag? Those Germans were always up to something new!

The late Geoff Halton, a much-missed colleague and long-time much-respected motoring correspondent of the *YEP*, is pictured here at the wheel of a 1910 Rover owned by a well-known Leeds enthusiast, Mr Arthur Lupton, of Whitkirk, who was a member of the Veteran Car Club. As they circle a roundabout, in August, 1858, let's plug in to what Geoff was thinking he would write: *

'Here I am driving one of the most immaculate old cars in Leeds. The Rover is great fun to drive and most satisfying. It engenders astonishing courtesy from other motorists. At tick-over, the firing strokes of the Knight sleeve valve single-cylinder engine can be counted. In the gate, the four gears are all in line and there is no foot throttle.

'The car chuffs happily along in top at 20mph and 33mpg for hour after hour, never having let Mr Lupton down yet. As with all old cars the brakes unnerved me. Adequate for the car's power and speed and any situation the driver might create, they evoke some anxiety in emergencies.'

You will gather that Geoff was the perfect gentlemen. Faced with a road rage situation, he would simply have apologised, taken one step back, raised his hat, re-entered his vehicle and driven off. Yes, those were the days!
* That is exactly what he wrote.

For many years this intriguing display atop the gate of the Autowrex Company at the junction of York Street and Marsh Lane, caused people to wonder what it was all about. As you might have guessed, it was simply a 'live' advertisement to draw attention to this source of cheap spares. But what about the two figures, the bunting and Union Flag?

In a letter to the editor of the *YEP*, Mr D. Lamb, of Paignton, Devon who was associated with Autowrex, wrote: 'The car was an early model Gladiator and the couple were intended as effigies of the then King and Queen" (Buckingham Palace must have been deeply appreciative).

'Around 1952 we changed the name of Autowrex to York Street Motors and, shortly afterwards, as the car and the tram lines on which it was mounted, started to crumble we took it down for safety's sake. In the end we swapped it for a saleable Jowett car, for which we eventually got £70. Eventually the Gladiator was bought by a Liverpool businessman who restored it to take part in veteran car rallies.'

(Sharp-eyed readers might have noted that spanning the space beneath the car is an aircraft propeller. Although Mr Lamb did not mention it, perhaps this came from an old biplane – believed to be an American Curtis 'Jenny' of US Air Mail fame – which had also graced the top of the gate for a period.)

In 1945, two De Dion veterans of the road (one of them pictured here), were found lying in the yard of Motor Wreckers of Leeds, and were bought by members of the Veteran Car Club of Great Britain, along with a Wolseley of turn-of-the-century vintage. All three had taken part in a veteran car rally from Leeds to Bradford and back in May 1931 the VCC had the idea of entering them in the first post-war London to Brighton Run.

The Wolseley (pictured before it was restored) went on to win the *Yorkshire Evening Post* silver cup in the 'Old Crocks Trial' during the Wakefield Centenary Week in June 1933. Producing about 8hp, it was chain-driven, had leather mudguards and every part of it was original. Just before World War Two, it was entered for the London to Brighton Run and taken to London but the race was cancelled and the vehicle remained there for three years. A spokesman for Motor Wreckers was quoted as saying that the Wolseley could achieved 30 to 35mph, but 'cornering at more than 15mph was asking for trouble'. The gears were a ticklish job, he added. It took him three days to find the four forward speeds, and three weeks to find the reverse gear. To move backwards it was necessary for the driver to stand up, take out the seat cushion and turn a handle tucked away there!

Also taking part in the Wakefield Centenary Pageant mentioned above was Mr A. Cope, of Sherburn-in-Elmete, photographed in his 1901 De Dion Bouton. Note the wary locals eyeing this Devilish device which obviously had some way to go before restoration was complete.

In these days when the establishment of car-building plants in someone else's country is a subject of much contention, it is interesting to note that there's nothing new in the game …and this story revolves around this Korte car of 1903.

But for fortune and, perhaps, a lack of capital, a German engineer might have launched a successful car factory in Leeds and we might have become the home of the Leedswagen. As far back as 1901 the engineer, Herr Korte, who was living in Leeds designed and built a car which was exhibited at London's Crystal Palace in 1902.

Unknown to Herr Korte, at the turn of the century, John William Woodhouse, of Leeds, made a great leap forward in the road transport business: he gave up his job as a steam traction engine driver and became the chauffeur of one of the new horseless carriages. It was, in fact, a 1903 model Korte owned by Mr L. Clayton, of a well-known Leeds family. In this 'before and after' photo, John William, wearing his chauffeur's cap and leggings, is at the wheel of the Korte; hoping he had left behind steam days – as defined by just a glimpse of a traction engine beyond the rear of the Korte. The picture, incidentally, was supplied by his son, John Woodhouse, who lives in Otley and produced it after a story on the Korte appeared in the *YEP* in 1991.

The Leeds-built Korte made a tremendous impression on visitors to the Crystal Palace. As you can see, it looked quite something on Stand 32; highly polished, and with a discreet notice in front reading: This Car is fitted with the new Dunlop Motor Tyres. The vehicle had an advanced specification for those days: the two-cylinder engine was water-cooled and there were four speeds and a reverse. But the car never had a definite name and there are arguments as to how many were built – 3 or 13? Herr Korte was bought out by Mr G. R. Rice and Mr Clayton who built some more cars at their Elland Road works. Three of them certainly remained in Yorkshire but are no longer in existence. What happened to the other(s) is not known.

Look closely, dear reader, at this superbly turned-out automobile, parked in all its glory in front of Leeds Civic Hall during the course of a sentimental journey to the city where, for years, it was parked in a prominent position. Have you got a clue to its identity? No? – then turn back to that picture of the car above the gate at Autowrex ...yes, it is the self-same machine – the 1902 Gladiator, registration U130, which was patiently restored by an Ellesmere Port motor trader, Mr Geoffrey Offley, who is seen in the car with Mrs Offley. They were taking part in the Veteran Car Club's Harrogate Rally of 1984 and were en route to Harrogate where there was to be a concours d'elegance on the Stray. The archive does not record if they won a prize, but they certainly deserved one.

The front of the Civic Hall seemed to be a popular pull-up for veteran cars and here's another – an 1899 Wolseley – driven by a veteran motorist, Mr St-John C. Nixon, then 74, who had taken part in the first RAC 1,000-mile Motor Trial in 1900, when an identical Wolseley was a winner in its class. This photograph was taken in May 1960, when Mr Nixon was being accompanied by his mechanic, Arthur Ayscough, on a Diamond Jubilee Run over a 1,000-mile course. And the lady? It was the then Lady Mayoress of Leeds, Mrs D. A. Stevenson, who popped out of the Civic Hall to see what all the fuss was about, and was promptly invited to step aboard to learn a few long-distance driving tips from the expert.

From the sublime to…

For the 'nobs' there was nothing very lofty or exalted about a motor tour in a 'chara', but if you had laboured in a mine all week, or a mill, or a clothing factory …then it could seem quite sublime to set off for a day out at the coast; or at one of those glorious Dales' hamlets.

Regretfully, in such a spot these days, if you want to take lunch you have to make a reservation sometime beforehand; or arrive by 11.30am at the latest to claim a table before fleets of ever-shiny BMW, Lexus, Rover, top-of-the-range Hondas etc, decant town-dwelling 'regulars' who start their 'starters' at 12 noon precisely; gnash rapidly through the rest and are fled the place by 1.30pm, thereby having no contact whatsoever with the locals, with whom a couple of pre-lunch pints can provide an insight into an entirely different way of life. You live and learn.

'Chara' trips started when a few thinking owners of early-model lorries realised (like the pioneer packaged holiday operators of the early 1950s), that expensive machinery can be better made to pay for itself if it is in near-constant use. So, on Friday nights, the lorry lads devised methods of removing the wagon backs that had carried goods all week, and replacing them with bodies equipped with rows of seats, a running board, a 'drop head' waterproof canopy and a driver with an official cap to take folks for a day/weekend out at the seaside; or wherever. Some owners could of course, afford custom-built coaches. Here's just such a group in the station yard at Scarborough, leaving for a trip to Bridlington in 1923. How adventurous could they get?

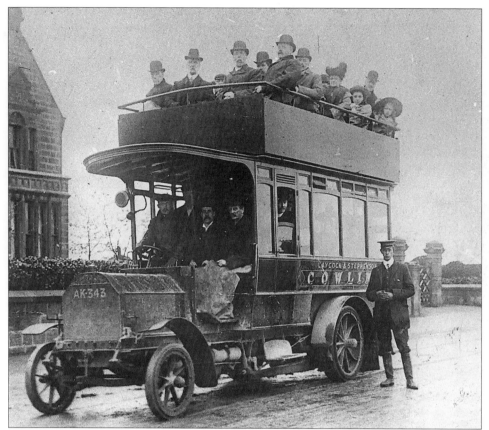

The bus/coach revolution did not, of course, simply come about for pleasure purposes. Eighty years ago the 'omnibus' – many of which had carried British Tommies to war in the 1914-18 conflict – was attracting the interest of transport companies of all shapes and sizes. It was not, as today, something to be cursed – by passengers when it does not turn up; or by other road users when too many of them jam the streets – for it was a blessing for town and country folk alike.

True enough, omnibus drivers sometimes had to perform major surgery on their engines – whatever the weather – to ribald comments when they were slow; and major cheers when the engine fired-up again. Buses, as they soon came to be known, often cut-out long walks at the beginning and end of exhausting shifts; they made family visits possible throughout the year, and wrought tremendous changes in housewives' shopping and social habits.

Like the Boeing Airplane Company in later years, the bus operators realised that two decks could carry more than one, thereby cutting the overheads and here is a group of pioneer passengers pictured on the trial run of one of Laycock and Stephenson's buses at Yeadon. The picture of them sampling the dubious comforts of an early bone-shaker was sent to the *YEP* by Mrs W. Flaxton, of Windmill Lane, Yeadon.

Few of the independent bus operators were quicker on the uptake than the ubiquitous Sammy Ledgard's, whose famous 'Blue Devils' turned-up in all manner of places. Mainly purchased second-hand from other companies, their buses provided a generally friendly 'hold tight and hope for the best' atmosphere; the drivers and conductors mixing-in well with the passengers because most never wore any form of uniform (as here). Some of their post-World War Two vehicles carried the nick-name 'striped backside makers', because the 'austerity' type vehicles, built with wooden slat seats during the war when there was shortage of textile materials, continued in service for many years afterwards and the effects, on passengers' buttocks, presumably, resulted in regular travellers coining the phrase.

Although Ledgard's appeared to concentrate on the regular bus service market, they were not averse to running evening, day or weekend outings – when, judging by this picture, some of their (ahem) ageing equipment was deemed fit for the revellers. As this group, pictured in the early 1920s, did not appear to have started revelling, one assumes this was the early-morning ready for-the-off pose: hence the overcoats and a fine assortment of headgear. One also assumes they were not going too far, for a note on the chassis says 'Speed 12M.P.H.' – but with a fair wind behind them, they could probably make it to York. Incidentally – is that Charlie Chaplin again at the wheel…?

No book on old Leeds would be complete without a picture of a tram. So here's No.28 of Leeds City Transport rocking and rolling toward Stanningley. Maybe this was a driver training run, for there appears to be a posse of uniformed figures both on the platform and in the upstairs verandah. On the other hand, maybe they were warders from Armley Jail searching for someone who had flown the nick …that establishment not being far from this possible line of escape.

Whatever the attractions of the Central Bus Station today, time was when this part of its predecessor was, well – the pits. About as attractive as a street snackbar when the temperature is around sixty below in Sverdlovsk, the graciously named Ladies Waiting Room struck horror into most women passengers and its 'modern' (oops!) lines, reminiscent of 'airport style' 1936, did nothing to conceal the hideous atmosphere of the interior, which was a regular cause for complaint in letters to the *YEP*. As a suitable ending to this section, lady readers may add whatever suitable words they can conjure-up to end the phrase that makes-up the heading on this section: From the sublime to…

Taking to the air

At a time when Leeds Bradford International Airport (LBA) is in the throes of construction and redevelopment work which will make it capable of handling ever-increasing numbers of passengers for some years to come, here's a look back at the then Yeadon Aerodrome before it even had a terminal: and not even the old white-painted clubhouse which served as one for several years around the 1950s. Pictured here is the old aeroplane club site at the west end of the then aerodrome in 1934 with Victoria Avenue coming just into the top left-hand corner of the picture. The 'semis' in the foreground were in a somewhat precarious position, one of them suffering the indignity, on 18 June 1939, of having a Hawker Hind biplane of No.609 (West Riding) Squadron, Auxiliary Air Force standing on its nose in the garden with its tailplane resting on the roof tiles. Wizard prang, chaps!

A sight like this today would be enough to give near-heart failure to LBA's Airside Operations and Safety Manager, Andy Barker. Taken from a spot roughly at the centre of the airside of today's terminal, this pre-World War Two photograph shows part of the enthusiastic crowd on the aerodrome to see a display by Hawker biplane day bombers of No.609 Squadron. Sensible footwear, fur coats, hats, caps, bowlers galore, plus-fours, children in school caps and blazers – yes, it was obviously a touch nippy that day but no one was looking sloppy: straight backs, firm jaws, polished engine cowlings – those were the days.

Thirty years on, and according to the original caption on this picture, written by some fellow named Rowley... 'This unusual sight on the parking apron at the Leeds and Bradford Airport yesterday will be a regular thing in the future as the airport develops. This is the first time so many large aircraft have been seen on the apron at one time.' Yes, it was quite exciting with, from left to right: two DC-3 Dakotas of BKS Air Transport; a Viscount of British European Airways; a Dart Herald an two Air Links Argonauts. They were parked on the apron in front of the huge flight shed (the black corner of which is on the left), which dominated the Yeadon skyline for many years. Originally, it was the place where near-completed Lancasters from the adjacent wartime aircraft factory had last adjustments made before flying off to their allocated RAF stations.

Time moves on and a few years later the old flight shed (which ended its days storing some 80,000 tons of fertiliser), had been demolished and the contents dispersed – fortunately for the residents and Bramhope, Cookridge and Adel, not to the four winds! Near where it had stood a new terminal building had arisen and on the apron passengers were boarding a British Midland Airways' Viscount; as ever clean and well-turned out. BM's latest generation jets continue to reflect this care.

With the decision taken to build Leeds Bradford's new long runway, allowing the airport to accept much larger aircraft which could operate long-haul flights, most of the airport area became a hive of activity; not least on Victoria Avenue (the main Bradford-Harrogate Road), which used to stand some 35ft above where this digger is standing, hard at work on preparations for the 240 metre tunnel which would in future carry the road under the new runway extension.

A helicopter's eye view, in September 1984, of the runway extension with its turning circle at the north-west end. The additional length it provided for take-offs and landings can be appreciated by comparing the new runway with LBA's old main runway – running from left to right just above the newly-extended apron area and the terminal buildings. Yeadon Tarn is right centre; the old Avro aircraft factory left centre; and houses at the bottom end of Cookridge i.e. near Cookridge Beck, just beyond the top left-hand corner. The Victoria Avenue tunnel under the runway extension is just to the right of the roundabout on the Bradford-Harrogate Road, almost in the centre of the photograph.

Bertie Boeing: "Wot's this 'ere then – causing me to stop dead when I've got right of way…?" Road Rage Rolls: "Hold your tongue, Sir, I'll have you know I have a lady of distinction aboard. Any more lip and her husband might just buy you out… you cheap kerosene-gulping monster…" But he already had – see next picture.

Yes, the 707 was the personal aircraft of Sheik Kamal Adham, the Saudi Arabian Foreign Minister whose wife, it was believed, had been brought to Leeds for specialist medical treatment. It was all a bit hush-hush. After the gleaming white Rolls had delivered its passengers back to the long-time parked aircraft, a group described as 'medical people' made their way back to the plane. No doubt they would have more leg room than sun-seeking holidaymakers boarding today's Boeing 707 successors; and the Saudis being off the stuff, there would be no chance of alcohol-induced air rage being generated as they headed back to Paris, from whence the aircraft came. Aye, it's all right for some...

Big brother Boeing – that runway extension certainly opened-up Leeds Bradford to bigger and better things. Not long after the author had won a bet with the then airport managing director, Gordon Dennison, that he would be the first person to step from a Jumbo jet onto LBA's apron; this other example of the Boeing Airplane Company's technical wizardry landed at LBA, in December 1984, and had the spotters all a-tremble.

Reason was that the aircraft was out on a photographic session 'over beautiful Yorkshire' to launch the classy new livery of British Airways. That livery preceded, of course, the 'oriental garden centre' look which now splatters the tail fins of BA aircraft; and which saw-off the Union Jack emblem, much to – rightly so – the consternation of retired colonels and Anglicised American tourists who 'wanted to fly British because it represents Britain, not some goddamn concoction thought-up by nutty designers.' And why did this semi-secret photographic session flight (involving two escorting camera-equipped jets and a helicopter), come to land at Leeds Bradford? Because it was flown by none other than Captain Michael Webster, the son of a Leeds couple, who had flown that very first Jumbo into the airport only a short time beforehand, and thought it would be ideal for landing and take-off shots; especially as Yorkshire formed the background to the aerial shots. Good on you, Mike! (Needless to say, since this was first written, British Airways has restored the Union Flag to some of its aircraft.)

Three years later, in April 1987, British Airways had another near-first at Leeds Bradford when another of their captains touched-down with the first BA Concorde to visit the airport. 'Near-first' incidentally, because Air France had beaten them to it with the first of a series of 'Faster than sound' supersonic flights over the North Sea. Despite this previous Gallic high-speed intrusion, the surrounds of the airport were near-buried in true-Brit enthusiasts when one of our own Concordes landed there for the first time. Here is just a small section of the crowd waiting to greet it on the south side of the airfield.

No, grandma, this wasn't Concorde. This curious contraption was thought-up by the aforementioned Gordon Dennison, a former LBA managing director, in-between answering a multitude of 'phone calls from irate residents of the leafy lanes of Horsforth and Menston, when they heard of his application to lift restrictions on operating hours at the airport. "Why", some of them cried (and especially their cohorts in Cookridge), "if planes start flying after ten at night they will drown out the noise from the Fox & Hounds, and the Eyrie and the Old Ball; and the motorbikes using Tinshill Road as Castle Donington; and the 40-ton trucks roaring round the back lanes to Bramhope. Life will never be the same again…"

'The Yeadon Flyer', as Mr Dennison's contraption was nick-named, original as ever; was his light-hearted response to the 'howls of protest' from those mentioned above. Bearing the slogan 'Open All Hours' and with the cunning registration G-024H – it was built by airport vehicle mechanics and took part in the Leeds Lord Mayor's Parade in June 1993. But should some irate Menston citizen take it into his head to destroy 'The Yeadon Flyer' where he thinks it now stands opposite the terminal building; I have a warning for him: don't use your head in the process – that one is made of brick.

Look up, look down – or you might miss it

The pace of life in today's world means that many of us have little or no time to stand and stare; or smell the roses, or even watch someone else working (which used to be a regular lunchtime past-time).

Which is a great pity, because in a city growing and changing at the pace of Leeds we miss many joys of the past; cannot wholly take-in the contribution some new buildings have made to the face of the city, or even remember what they replaced – in some cases only a few months previously.

However, the iron discipline of getting-up early on a Sunday morning, driving down near empty roads to the city centre, parking the car then taking a perambulation around streets, squares, alleys and what-have-you, in order to check-out various items and locations, turned into voyages of discovery for the author (who thought he knew a great deal about the 'Old String of Beads' as *Yorkshire Evening Post* van drivers nick-named the city years ago). And early Sunday is one of the few times when it is possible to stand and stare; to look up, or down, without worrying over-much about the traffic, or being mugged.

On the 'up' side, there are some fascinating carvings on many buildings in the city centre – especially in Park Row (but catch them soon before glass-walled structures replace them); and also take to the bridges to look around and see how much the riverside has opened-up. Meanwhile here are a few other items, old and (fairly) new, that might intrigue you…

Oddities, Curiosities and suchlike

When the author was working as aviation correspondent of *The Journal*, in Edmonton, Alberta, it was a recognised thing that you knew on what date the first big snowfall of the previous autumn had occurred when, in the following (late) spring, ice on the sidewalks began to melt, revealing occasional copies of *The Journal* bearing the date when some sliding pedestrians had dropped them. He was reminded of this when, in a dark corner of the YEP archives, he stumbled over a pile of old newspapers, the top one of which turned out to be a copy of the *Yorkshire Post* and *Leeds Mercury* of Friday, 30 January 1942 and bore this picture (above) of a one-horse-power snow plough working in City Square the previous day.

Mr Harry Haley, of the Leeds Corporation Works Department, found himself with quite a ticklish job in City Square in June 1970, when he used abrasive measures to clean up the, ahem! torso of one of the famous nymphs. As far as we can see, Harry didn't bat an eyelid behind his mask; nor did the nymph get any of the publicity which followed the revelation of a famous film star's unshaven armpit, at a new film launch in spring 1999.

Still in City Square: as you can see, you have to hand it to Dr Walter Hook, a famed Vicar of Leeds and champion of workers' rights, for he has got to grips with another social cause. This time some wag had set up his silent protest about no-parking areas, which were to be marked out in July 1978. Not of great concern to the vicar in the centre of the square, you might have thought... But someone put him up to it, and the 'poor people's parson' could never resist a good cause. The hand grasping the cone was seen as a warning gesture to traffic wardens; and had they lived in his day, they would certainly have been foolish to incur the wrath of the belligerent, stubborn Dr Hook – perhaps Leeds's greatest vicar.

Far from the buzz of City Square, lonely Ethel Preston stands before her ever-open door in Lawnswood Cemetery. This monument, where the city's urban areas finally give way to the countryside and the glorious prospect of the Dales, is well-known; but little is known about its unique design or purpose. The cemetery was opened in 1876 and it is the understanding of the present staff that soon after Ethel's marriage, her husband died. Before she too passed away, it seems she expressed the wish that behind the statue which was to depict her, seemingly still comparatively young, there should be a pair of double doors, with one left slightly ajar so that her husband could rejoin her. "It's a real mystery," said one of the staff. But what a nice thought.

This timber-framed structure of part of a medieval manor house was found in property off Beeston Hill – arguably Holbeck say some residents – and is believed to be the oldest ecclesiastical building in the city.

Non-Leeds readers will have noted the references to 'Loiners' throughout this volume and the standard explanation that it refers to folks born and bred in the city. But there are also those of another persuasion who think the name is a corruption of the name of the big cats which guard the approaches to the Town Hall, as pictured here. One thing is certain, it would be less risky trying to feed one of the Town Hall 'lions' by hand than it would some strident 'Loiners' – especially on a day when, heaven forbid, Leeds United at had lost at home.

It could be that the favourite song of Mr John Waugh, a stores assistant at the Yorkshire Water Authority Harehills Depot, was *Singing in the Rain* as he checked-out the huge stock of standpipes on the premises in June 1976. He would know full well that the authority was the (water) butt of many jokes and hackneyed phrases: especially the popular one after two successive days of sunshine: "Bet yond watter lot can't wait to get them stand-pipes up."

Now then, where was I? is what the impressive statue of the explorer Stephen Cabot seems to indicate he's thinking as he examines a hand-held globe of the world as he knew it. At one time the statue graced the old Royal Exchange Building at the corner of Park Row and Boar Lane but was removed in the 1920s. It was later rescued from a builder's yard and re-erected in the garden of a house at Roundhay; not all that far from another garden where a lion which once topped a Leeds brewery entrance ended-up. But being an explorer, Cabot was probably used to that sort of company.

Driving along Dewsbury Road (or what's left of it) these days is just about as far removed from medieval times as you could possibly get – apart from the potholes for which Leeds is establishing something of a reputation. So it was all to the credit of the City Council, along with the Royal Institute of British Architects and the Leeds Permanent Building Society, that back in 1991 they set up the Leeds Awards for Architecture. And Stank Hall Barn, off Dewsbury Road, whose interior is pictured, had undergone essential repairs to its roof and walls to make it a favourite in the altered buildings category. The Grade II listed building was developed from a yeoman's farm complex in the 12th century and was known historically as the Farnley Woods Plot. Rebuilt in the 17th century, it was possibly the site of a secret nonconformist chapel.

Set into the wall of a former stable in Crown Court, a narrow alley running from Kirkgate to the Corn Exchange, these two carved stone skulls are said to commemorate two men who were press-ganged into the army. They were made to sleep on straw on the site, and possibly sank too well into it, for both suffocated during the night.

And now for a very curious curiosity indeed: back in 1991, a postcard competition to find the world's most boring view brought a howl of protest from proud Leeds. For a postcard (pictured) submitted by a Sussex man, and entitled: 'View of the gasworks, from Addington Street toilets, Leeds' won second place in the national contest with attracted 5,000 entries from all over the world. Commented Mr Stan Kenyon, then Leeds Director of Planning: "It gives an utterly ridiculous, negative and outdated image of the city at a crucial time in its economic development." Apparently no spokesman was available for the toilet users…

Leeds from Aloft

With so many people we know flying off on holidays here, there and everywhere, readers might find it surprising it is not all that many years since only 14 per cent of the British public had ever flown.

From that situation we have progressed rapidly to a position where not only are passenger figures increasing month by month at Leeds Bradford International Airport, but as residents in districts around the airport are well aware, the learning to fly business is also enjoying something of a boom and, at weekends in particular, light aircraft are rarely out of the sky for long.

Despite all this aerial activity, a large percentage of the citizens of Leeds haven't the slightest idea what the city looks like from the air. After all, if you are strapped in a seat in the middle row of an Airbus or Boeing 767 en route to or from Tenerife, there's not much chance of seeing what's happening down in The Headrow: unless the pilot puts his plane into a highly-undesirable manoeuvre which is highly unlikely!

So the author selected these aerial pictures that not only bring to light Leeds from aloft, they also illustrate how the city is continually changing; and provide new angles on familiar locations which simply cannot be obtained on the ground. And aerial views are very revealing: when flying as an aviation correspondent years ago, the author was constantly surprised by the number of houses in Wharfedale and on the Plain of York which were equipped with outdoor swimming pools. And as a well-known character with the RAF's Air Sea Rescue Unit at Leconfield used to say: "Flying a helicopter emphasises that in the privacy of their own back gardens the English are anything but reserved..."

Easily identified landmarks in this March 1988 photograph are the Civic Hall (top left), Town Hall (right of centre at top), the new Crown Court complex (right centre) and the mass of Leeds General Infirmary buildings taking up most of the centre of the picture. The aircraft from which this picture was taken would have been just about over Little Woodhouse Street. St George's Church is just below the centre on the right.

In August 1967, this splendid panorama was obtained by a photographer in an aircraft passing over the general area of Richmond Hill; from where the first illustration in this book (the drawing on Page 10) was made in 1745. The 32-year-old view pictured here shows The Headrow and Eastgate coming diagonally across the picture from top left (with the Town Hall marked by a No.2); past the crossing with Briggate at the Odeon Cinema (No.4), to decant in front of Quarry Hill Flats; almost all of which appear in the area marked No.1. Number 3 indicates the Civic Hall, No.6 marks the line of the Inner Ring Road, with Woodhouse Lane and Blenheim Walk to left and right of the number. Number 5 marks the Merrion Street multi-storey car park; No.7 the Central Bus Station and No.8 the Markets area. The Leeds to York railway line runs diagonally across the bottom of the photo. Picture: C. H. Wood (Bradford) Ltd.

This photograph was taken on 9 March 1970, from an aircraft flying over the Little London and Woodhouse areas; looking south/south-west. Claypit Lane comes in from the bottom left-hand corner and then crosses over the Inner Ring Road which, as it goes off to the right, passes under the then under-construction multi-storey car park. A great deal of demolition had taken place in the districts throughout the bottom half of the picture. Carlton Gate, still more or less intact, runs across the very bottom. The Merrion Centre is just above left-centre and cleared areas still to be developed can be seen near the Woodhouse Lane – Cookridge Street junction. The Town Hall is near the top of the picture, just to the left of centre.

Next page:

In this view, looking north-east, and taken from an aircraft over Park Lane in January 1987, the city's road system stands out well following a snowfall. A prominent feature is the roundabout at the start of Westgate in the right foreground, with the Brotherton House police offices to its right. To the left of the roundabout, the Inner Ring Road emerges from the tunnel which runs under it; and the now demolished Telecom House is just in front of where the south end of the tunnel emerges to the right of the roundabout. The block of flats in the bottom right-hand corner is Marlborough Towers. Looking up the picture from the roundabout: Westgate, The Headrow and Eastgate run in sequence and almost in a straight line to a snow-covered open space which is where Quarry Hill Flats used to stand. Just to the right of the end of Eastgate, the large dark-coloured building is Millgarth police station. The Town Hall is almost in the centre of the picture with the Civic Hall at left centre and the Leeds Infirmary complex just below it from this angle.

Near-surrounded today by swirling 24-hour traffic; on 24 July 1989, work was going on apace on more developments around the impressive new ASDA headquarters on the south bank of the River Aire, which runs across the centre of the picture. The Victoria Bridge is on the left and the Hilton National Leeds City hotel at the very top, left of centre. A good deal of construction work was going on across the road from the Hilton National,

but work had yet to start on the ultra-modern building which now dominates the former coal loading stage between the Hilton National and the river. Sovereign Street (just above the light-coloured roof on the right) has the sad remains of the Queens Hall complex, formerly the city's main tram depot where the last bell was clanged and the last sock removed from a driver's control handle long, long ago…

Subscribers

Roger J Ackroyd
Janet Aldridge
Stephen Allinson
Mrs Margaret Alnwick
V Armitage
Dennis Uttley Astin
M B Bailey
Keith Baker
Malcolm G Barker OBE
Betty Barlow
Peter Bastow
Barry & Margaret Bellhouse
Janet Blackburn
Avril Blum
Paul Bolton
Mr Walter Brock
Peter G Brogden
Linda M Bromby
S Brown
Peter G Buckland
Gordon L Caleb
Mr James Cheetham
Peter A Childs
Dennis M Cowen
Mr & Mrs Crabtree
Irving Crawford
Cross Flatts Park Primary School
Peter John Cunnane
C J Cusworth
Mrs M Dawes
Ann Dawson
Peter Dealtry
Gordon Dick
Alan Dickinson
Mrs A Dresser
Sally Evans
Mr J Fairburn
D Falkingham
Keith Feeney
Mrs B M Finch
V Finkle
John Foster
Harry Fowler
Gemma Fox
John & Lillian Garlick
Mrs Sheila Gaunt
A Gillon
Peter Gilson
Rose Green
Garry John Hall
Joan Harrison
Mrs J A Hartley
M A Hayton
Mrs Shirley Heald
Jim & Eunice Hudson
Robert Hughes
Mrs M Indriksons

Hilary Ineson
Muriel Johnson
Pete & June Jones
Elsie Kelly
Clifford Lackey
Mr H Levey
Steven Lunn
Trevor Lyons
Mrs L Mackintosh
Mrs Bernice McManus
Anthony Metcalfe
Eric & Barbara Noble
D Palfreyman
Roy Pickering
Stephen R Pickering
Mr & Mrs J & M Pitts
Mrs P Rae
Robert E Redman
Mr T Reynolds
Mr W Reynolds
John Rhodes
Howard Ripley
George Richards
Colin Roberts
R Sanderson
Robert Sherburn
Eric P Simpson
Nora Sixsmith
Dorothy M Smalley
G W Smith
John & Joan Smith
Nina Smith
J M Spink
Phyllis Stead
Mr F R A Stirk
Mr A Stubbs
Muriel Sunderland
M R Swift
Elaine Taylor
Mrs K Taylor
S M Thomas
Keith Thompson
E M & J Todd
Mr D M Tranter
M F Vedere
Dennis Waddle
Colin Waite
Neil A Wallace
Andrew Charles Watson
Mrs I Watson
Les Watson
Ian Webber
Mrs K Wilcox
Barrie Williamson
Harry Wood
J E Wright